# National Compensation Survey: Employee Benefits in Private Industry in the United States, 2000

U.S. Department of Labor
Elaine L. Chao, Secretary

Bureau of Labor Statistics
Kathleen P. Utgoff, Commissioner

January 2003

Bulletin 2555

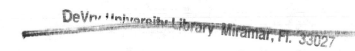

# Preface

This bulletin presents findings of the 2000 Bureau of Labor Statistics (BLS) survey of the incidence of selected employee benefit plans in private industry establishments and detailed provisions of health care and retirement income plans. Data in this bulletin are from the National Compensation Survey and replace publications known as Employee Benefits in Medium and Large Private Establishments, Employee Benefits in Small Private Establishments, and Employee Benefits in State and Local Governments. Future publications of benefits data will include all private industry and State and local government establishments.

The public may access Employee Benefits Survey data through the Bureau of Labor Statistics' World Wide Web site at **http://www.bls.gov/ncs/home.htm**. Questions on the data in this publication should be referred to the staff of the National Compensation Survey at (202) 606-6199 or via E-mail: *OCLTINFO@bls.gov*. Sensory impaired individuals may obtain information in this publication upon request. Voice phone: (202) 691-5200; Federal Relay Service: 1-800-877-8339.

# Contents

# Contents—Continued

# Contents—Continued

# Chapter 1.  Results of the 2000 Survey

Paid time off was the most prevalent benefit available to workers in private establishments in 2000. Paid vacations were available to 80 percent of employees and paid holidays to 77 percent of employees in private industry.

In 2000, 52 percent of employees in private industry participated in medical care plans. Forty-eight percent were covered by retirement benefits of at least one type, either a defined benefit plan (19 percent) or a defined contribution plan (36 percent), with approximately 7 percent of employees enrolled in both types of plans. Life insurance was available to over half of all employees in private industry. Short- and long-term disability benefits were less common; they were available to 34 and 26 percent of employees, respectively.

Other benefits frequently offered in private industry include non-production bonuses (offered to 48 percent of employees) and work-related educational assistance (available to 38 percent). Among benefits less often available to employees were severance pay (available to 20 percent of employees), job-related travel accident insurance (15 percent), and long-term care insurance (7 percent).

Of the 52 percent of private sector workers with medical care coverage, premiums were fully paid by the employer for 32 percent of those with single coverage plans and 19 percent of those with family coverage. The majority of medical plan participants were required to contribute a flat monthly amount, averaging $54.40 for single coverage and $179.75 for family coverage.

Access to most benefits, as well as the availability of fully paid medical care and the amount of required contributions to the cost of medical care, varied by worker and establishment characteristics.

## Worker characteristics

Benefits coverage varied by occupational group, full- and part-time status, and union and nonunion status. Of the three occupational groups for which data are presented, professional, technical, and related employees generally had the greatest incidence of coverage. Retirement benefits covered 66 percent of professional, technical, and related employees, compared with 50 percent of clerical and sales employees and 39 percent of blue-collar and service employees.

Payment of premiums for medical care coverage also varied by employee characteristics. Thirty-eight percent of blue-collar and service workers covered by medical care benefits had their coverage fully paid for by their employers, compared with 25 percent of professional, technical, and related employees and 28 percent of clerical and sales employees.

## Establishment characteristics

Benefit incidence varied by establishment employment size. For example, 65 percent of workers in establishments with 100 employees or more (medium and large establishments) were covered by retirement benefits compared with 33 percent of employees in small establishments (those with fewer than 100 workers). The difference in coverage for paid time off benefits was smaller: 86 percent of employees in medium and large establishments had paid holiday benefits, for example, compared with 70 percent in small establishments.

The incidence of fully paid coverage for medical care was similar in small establishments to that in medium and large establishments. Average monthly employee contributions for single coverage averaged $60.12 in small establishments and $49.56 in medium and large establishments.

Coverage for benefits also varied by industry. Retirement benefits covered 57 percent of workers in goods-producing industries, compared with 45 percent in service-producing industries. Long-term disability coverage also was more widespread in goods-producing industries, covering 31 percent of employees compared with 24 percent of employees in service-producing industries. Short-term disability benefits covered 45 percent of employees in goods-producing industries and 30 percent of those in service-producing industries.

# Definitions

## Paid holidays

Holidays are days of special religious, cultural, or patriotic significance on which work and business ordinarily ceases. Workers typically receive time-off from work, at full or partial pay, for a specified number of holidays each year. Some employers also include "personal holidays," such as an employee's birthday or "floating holidays" that vary from year-to-year as determined by the employer or employee. When a holiday falls on a scheduled day off, such as a Saturday or Sunday, another day off is often substituted. The following are typical paid holidays:

New Years Day;
Memorial Day;
Independence Day;
Labor Day;
Thanksgiving Day; and
Christmas Day.

## Paid vacations

Vacations are time-off from work, normally taken in days or weeks. Vacation benefits usually start after a length-of-service requirement is fulfilled. The amount of time-off may vary based on an employee's service with the employer or it may be a fixed number of days per year. The time-off is usually paid at an employee's normal hourly rate or salary.

## Disability benefits

*Short-term disability (STD)* benefits provide for salary replacement, most often partial pay, for a 6- to 12- month period. Benefits are either paid as a percentage of employee earnings, such as 50 percent of pre-disability earnings, or a flat dollar amount. STD benefits can vary by the amount of pre-disability earnings, length of service with the establishment, or length of disability.

*Long-term Disability (LTD)* benefits provide a monthly cash amount to eligible employees who, due to illness or injury, are unable to work for an extended period of time. Benefits are usually paid as a fixed percent of pre-disability earnings up to a set limit. Most participants have a waiting period of 3 or 6 months, or until sick leave and STD benefits end, before benefit payments begin. LTD payments generally continue until retirement, a specified age, or for a period that varies by the employee's age at the time of disability.

## Survivor benefits

*Life insurance* provides a benefit in the event of death or dismemberment. Benefits are usually distributed as a lump sum but can also be paid out in the form of an annuity.

*Accidental death and dismemberment insurance (AD&D).* Often referred to as double indemnity, this type of life insurance plan provides benefits to the employee or the employee's beneficiary in the event of accidental death or bodily dismemberment. The AD&D benefit commonly equals the basic life insurance benefit in the case of death and a portion of the life benefit for dismemberment.

*Survivor income benefits* provide a monthly income to surviving members of a deceased employee's family. These benefits are in addition to other benefits, such as basic life insurance and survivor pension benefits. Survivor income payments are generally a percentage of the employee's pay or a flat dollar amount. Benefits usually continue for 24 months, although some continue until a specific event occurs, such as the surviving spouse remarries or reaches age 65, or surviving children reach a given age.

**Educational assistance benefits** provide to the employee full or partial payment for tuition, books, or other related expenses. This benefit can be of two categories: (1) general knowledge that is non-work related or (2) particular knowledge or skills that are work-related.

**Subsidized commuting** provides full or partial payment for the cost of an employee's commute to work via public transportation, a company sponsored van pool, discount subway fares, or bus tokens. Use of a company car does not qualify as subsidized commuting.

## Non-wage cash benefits

*Nonproduction cash bonuses* are cash payments outside of regular pay or commissions to employees as part of an established practice or a formal plan that is based upon factors such as attainment of general goals.

*Supplemental Unemployment Benefits,* financed by the employer, provide weekly payments that supplement State unemployment insurance payments given to laid-off employees or employees with shortened work weeks. These plans are almost always found in the auto and steel industries.

*Severance pay* is a lump sum or installment cash payment made to employees permanently separated from the company. Severance pay also includes technological severance pay: pay given to employees permanently separated from employment due to technological changes or plant closings.

**Travel accident insurance** provides payments in the event of the death or injury of an employee who is traveling on company business. Travelers insurance is a specific form of accidental death and dismemberment insurance.

## Family benefits

*Child care* provides for the cost, either fully or partially, of caring for an employee's children in a nursery, day care center, or by a baby-sitter. Provided care can be in facilities either on or off the employer's premises.

*Adoption assistance* provides financial aid to reimburse all or part of the cost of adopting a child.

*Long-term care insurance* pays full or partial benefits for long-term (more than one year) custodial care, extended to active employees, retirees, parents of active employees, or to dependents of active employees and retirees.

## Health promotion programs

*Wellness programs* are independent of health insurance plans and offer employees two or more of the following benefits:

- Smoking cessation clinics
- Exercise/physical fitness programs
- Weight control programs
- Nutrition education
- Hypertension tests
- Periodic physical examinations
- Stress management courses
- Back care courses
- Life style assessment tests

*Fitness centers*, financed in whole or part by the employer, either on or off the work site.

**Flexible work place** is a formal program that allows employees who would otherwise work at the establishment to work either some or all of their work schedule at home.

---

### A Note on the Tables

The majority of the tables presented throughout this bulletin indicate the percent of all employees, or of a selected group of employees, covered by particular benefits and benefit features. Understanding the group of employees about whom data are being presented is the key to using these tables; this information is contained in the first row of each table. Some tables indicate the percent of all employees covered by the survey who have a certain benefit; other tables show the percent of employees covered by a certain benefit who have a certain plan feature. Rows where there are no participants reported are deleted from the tables.

For example, table 1 indicates that 51 percent of all full-time employees were covered by a medical care plan. In chapter 2, most of the tables present data on the percent of full-time workers with medical care who are in plans with certain provisions. Workers with medical care equal 100 percent in these tables, with smaller percentages indicating the availability of plan features. For example, in table 14, 100 percent refers to those workers with medical care plans, and 9 percent indicates those workers with medical care covered by a traditional fee-for-service plan.

Another type of table estimate presented throughout the bulletin displays average benefit values rather than percentages of workers. These averages are presented for all covered workers; averages exclude workers without the plan provision.

Data calculations are discussed in more detail in the appendices.

**Table 1. Summary: Participation in selected employee benefit programs, full-time and part-time employees, private industry, National Compensation Survey, 2000**

(In percent)

| Benefit | All employees | Profes- sional, technical, and related employees | Clerical and sales employees | Blue-collar and service employ- ees |
|---|---|---|---|---|
| Paid time off: | | | | |
| Holidays ............................................. | 77 | 84 | 80 | 72 |
| Vacations ........................................... | 80 | 87 | 80 | 77 |
| Disability benefits[1]: | | | | |
| Short-term disability ........................ | 33 | 49 | 32 | 27 |
| Long-term disability insurance ........ | 25 | 50 | 27 | 14 |
| Survivor benefits: | | | | |
| Life insurance ................................. | 54 | 75 | 52 | 47 |
| Accidental death and dismemberment .......................... | 41 | 58 | 38 | 36 |
| Survivor income benefits .............. | 2 | 3 | 2 | 2 |
| Health care benefits: | | | | |
| Medical care ................................... | 51 | 63 | 50 | 47 |
| Dental care ..................................... | 29 | 42 | 29 | 24 |
| Vision care ...................................... | 17 | 24 | 17 | 15 |
| Outpatient prescription drug coverage ...................................... | 49 | 61 | 47 | 45 |
| Retirement income benefits: | | | | |
| All retirement[2] .................................... | 48 | 65 | 49 | 39 |
| Defined benefit ............................. | 19 | 26 | 18 | 17 |
| Defined contribution[3] .................... | 36 | 52 | 40 | 26 |
| Savings and thrift ....................... | 26 | 41 | 27 | 20 |
| Deferred profit sharing .............. | 8 | 10 | 10 | 5 |
| Employee stock ownership ....... | 2 | 2 | 3 | 1 |
| Money purchase pension ......... | 4 | 6 | 5 | 2 |
| Stock bonus ............................. | (⁴) | (⁴) | (⁴) | (⁴) |
| Simplified employee pension .... | 1 | 1 | 1 | 1 |
| Cash or deferred arrangements: | | | | |
| With employer contributions ..... | 30 | 47 | 31 | 22 |
| No employer contributions ........ | 10 | 15 | 10 | 8 |

[1] The definitions for paid sick leave and short-term disability (previously sickness and accident insurance) were changed for the 1995 survey. Paid sick leave now only includes plans that either specify a maximum number of days per year or unlimited days. Short-term disability now includes all insured, self-insured, and state-mandated plans available on a per disability basis as well as the unfunded per disability plans previously reported as sick leave. Sickness and accident insurance, reported in years prior to the 1995 survey, only included insured, self-insured, and state-mandated plans providing per disability benefits at less than full pay.
[2] Includes defined benefit pension plans and defined contribution retirement plans. The total is less than the sum of the individual items because many employees participated in both types of plans.
[3] The total is less than the sum of the individual items because some employees participated in more than one type of plan.
[4] Less than 0.5 percent.

NOTE: Because of rounding, sums of individual items may not equal totals. Where applicable, dash indicates that no data were reported.

**Table 2. Other benefits: Eligibility for specified benefits, full-time and part-time employees, private industry, National Compensation Survey, 2000**
(In percent)

| Benefit | All employees | Profes-sional, technical, and related employees | Clerical and sales employees | Blue-collar and service employees |
|---|---|---|---|---|
| **Income continuation plans:** | | | | |
| Severance pay ...................... | 20 | 35 | 24 | 12 |
| Supplemental unemployment benefits ............................. | 1 | 1 | 1 | 1 |
| **Family benefits:** | | | | |
| Employer assistance for child care ................................... | 4 | 11 | 5 | 2 |
| Employer provided funds .. | 2 | 4 | 3 | 1 |
| On-site child care ............. | 2 | 6 | 1 | 1 |
| Off-site child care ............. | 1 | 3 | 2 | ($^{1}$) |
| Adoption assistance ............ | 5 | 12 | 5 | 2 |
| Long-term care insurance ..... | 7 | 14 | 7 | 4 |
| Flexible workplace ................ | 5 | 12 | 4 | 1 |
| **Health promotion programs:** | | | | |
| Wellness programs .............. | 18 | 35 | 17 | 11 |
| Fitness center ...................... | 9 | 19 | 10 | 4 |
| **Miscellaneous benefits:** | | | | |
| Job-related travel accident insurance ........................... | 15 | 30 | 15 | 9 |
| Nonproduction bonuses ........ | 48 | 52 | 48 | 46 |
| Subsidized commuting ......... | 3 | 6 | 3 | 2 |
| **Education assistance:** | | | | |
| Job-related ........................ | 38 | 62 | 37 | 28 |
| Not job-related .................. | 9 | 19 | 8 | 8 |

[1] Less than 0.5 percent.

NOTE: Because of rounding, sums of individual items may not equal totals. Where applicable, dash indicates that no data were reported.

**Table 3. Medical care benefits: Percent of participants required to contribute and average employee contribution, private industry, National Compensation Survey,[1] 2000**

| Characteristics | Single Coverage | | | Family Coverage | | |
|---|---|---|---|---|---|---|
| | Employee contributions not required | Employee contributions required | Average[2] flat monthly contribution in dollars | Employee contributions not required | Employee contributions required | Average[2] flat monthly contribution in dollars |
| Total ............................................ | 32 | 68 | $54.40 | 19 | 81 | $179.75 |
| **Worker characteristics:[3]** | | | | | | |
| Professional, technical, and related employees[4] .............................. | 25 | 75 | 54.32 | 15 | 85 | 183.51 |
| Clerical and sales employees[4] ............ | 28 | 72 | 54.14 | 16 | 84 | 187.07 |
| Blue-collar and service employees[4] ..... | 38 | 62 | 54.63 | 23 | 77 | 172.69 |
| Union ............................................. | – | – | – | – | – | – |
| Nonunion ........................................ | 27 | 73 | 55.63 | 13 | 87 | 185.79 |
| Full time ......................................... | 31 | 69 | 53.93 | 19 | 81 | 180.16 |
| Part time ........................................ | – | – | – | – | – | – |
| **Establishment characteristics:** | | | | | | |
| Goods-producing ............................. | 36 | 64 | 57.59 | 25 | 75 | 189.76 |
| Service-producing ............................ | 30 | 70 | 53.34 | 17 | 83 | 176.41 |
| 1-99 workers ................................... | 34 | 66 | 60.12 | 19 | 81 | 182.32 |
| 100 workers or more ......................... | 30 | 70 | 49.56 | 20 | 80 | 177.47 |

[1] The survey covers all 50 States and the District of Columbia. Collection was conducted between February and December 2000. The average reference period was July 2000.

[2] The average is presented for all covered workers and excludes workers without the plan provision. Averages are for plans stating a flat monthly cost.

[3] Employees are classified as working either a full-time or part-time schedule based on the definition used by each establishment. Union workers are those whose wages are determined through collective bargaining.

[4] A classification system including about 480 individual occupations is used to cover all workers in the civilian economy. See the Technical Note for more information.

NOTE: Because of rounding, sums of individual items may not equal totals. Where applicable, dash indicates no employees in this category or data do not meet publication criteria.

**Table 4. Medical care benefits: Percent of participants, by amount and type of employee contribution for individual coverage, private industry, National Compensation Survey,[1] 2000**

| Type and amount of contribution | All employees | Professional, technical, and related employees[2] | Clerical and sales employees[2] | Blue-collar and service employees[2] |
|---|---|---|---|---|
| Number with contributory coverage (in thousands) ......... | 37,961 | 10,913 | 11,306 | 15,742 |
| | Percent | | | |
| Total with contributory coverage | 100 | 100 | 100 | 100 |
| Flat monthly amount ............. | 79 | 76 | 77 | 81 |
| Less than $5.00 ................. | ($^3$) | ($^3$) | 1 | ($^3$) |
| $5.00 - 9.99 ...................... | 2 | 3 | 1 | 1 |
| $10.00 - 14.99 .................. | 3 | 3 | 4 | 3 |
| $15.00 - 19.99 .................. | 6 | 7 | 5 | 7 |
| $20.00 - 29.99 .................. | 11 | 10 | 9 | 12 |
| $30.00 - 39.99 .................. | 13 | 12 | 13 | 15 |
| $40.00 - 49.99 .................. | 12 | 15 | 11 | 12 |
| $50.00 - 59.99 .................. | 6 | 6 | 9 | 4 |
| $60.00 - 69.99 .................. | 5 | 3 | 5 | 6 |
| $70.00 - 79.99 .................. | 5 | 3 | 5 | 6 |
| $80.00 - 89.99 .................. | 4 | 3 | 4 | 4 |
| $90.00 - 99.99 ................. | 1 | ($^3$) | 1 | 1 |
| $100.00 - 124.99 ............. | 3 | 2 | 3 | 4 |
| $125.00 or greater ........ | 7 | 10 | 5 | 7 |
| Dollar amount unspecified | ($^3$) | ($^3$) | ($^3$) | ($^3$) |
| Composite rate[4] ................... | 2 | 3 | 2 | 3 |
| Varies[5] ................................. | 5 | 5 | 5 | 4 |
| Flexible benefits[6] ................. | 8 | 12 | 7 | 7 |
| Percent of earnings ............. | ($^3$) | ($^3$) | – | ($^3$) |
| Exists, but unknown ............. | 6 | 4 | 9 | 5 |

[1] The survey covers all 50 States and the District of Columbia. Collection was conducted between February and December 2000. The average reference period was July 2000.

[2] A classification system including about 480 individual occupations is used to cover all workers in the civilian economy. See the Technical Note for more information.

[3] Less than 0.5 percent

[4] A composite rate is a set contribution covering more than one benefit area, for example, health care and life insurance. Cost data for individual plans cannot be determined.

[5] Based on worker attributes. For example, employee contributions may vary based on earnings, length of service, or age.

[6] Amount varies by options selected under a "cafeteria plan" or employer-sponsored reimbursement account.

NOTE: Because of rounding, sums of individual items may not equal totals. Where applicable, dash indicates no employees in this category.

**Table 5. Medical care benefits: Percent of participants, by amount and type of employee contribution for family coverage,[1] private industry, National Compensation Survey,[2] 2000**

| Type and amount of contribution | All employees | Professional, technical, and related employees[3] | Clerical and sales employees[3] | Blue-collar and service employees[3] |
|---|---|---|---|---|
| Number (in thousands) with contributory coverage ............ | 44,822 | 12,276 | 13,207 | 19,338 |
| | Percent | | | |
| Total with contributory coverage | 100 | 100 | 100 | 100 |
| Flat monthly amount ............ | 81 | 79 | 80 | 84 |
| Less than $20.00 ............ | 1 | 1 | 1 | 1 |
| $20.00 - 29.99 ................ | 2 | 2 | 2 | 2 |
| $30.00 - 39.99 ................ | 2 | 2 | 1 | 3 |
| $40.00 - 49.99 ................ | 2 | 3 | 1 | 2 |
| $50.00 - 59.99 ................ | 4 | 3 | 3 | 5 |
| $60.00 - 69.99 ................ | 3 | 3 | 2 | 3 |
| $70.00 - 79.99 ................ | 4 | 4 | 3 | 4 |
| $80.00 - 89.99 ................ | 5 | 5 | 4 | 4 |
| $90.00 - 99.99 ................ | 3 | 3 | 3 | 3 |
| $100.00 - 124.99 ............ | 9 | 10 | 10 | 8 |
| $125.00 - 149.99 ............ | 5 | 6 | 7 | 4 |
| $150.00 - 174.99 ............ | 10 | 8 | 10 | 12 |
| $175.00 - 199.99 ............ | 5 | 3 | 4 | 6 |
| $200.00 - 224.99 ............ | 4 | 5 | 3 | 4 |
| $225.00 - 249.99 ............ | 3 | 2 | 4 | 3 |
| $250.00 - 274.99 ............ | 5 | 3 | 6 | 5 |
| $275.00 - 299.99 ............ | 3 | 1 | 4 | 3 |
| $300.00 or greater ............ | 13 | 15 | 13 | 11 |
| Composite rate[4] .................... | 2 | 2 | 1 | 2 |
| Varies[5] ................................. | 4 | 5 | 5 | 4 |
| Flexible benefits[6] ................ | 7 | 11 | 6 | 6 |
| Percent of earnings ............. | ([7]) | ([7]) | – | ([7]) |
| Exists, but unknown ............. | 5 | 3 | 8 | 4 |

[1] If the amount of contribution varied by either size or composition of family, the rate for an employee with a spouse and one child was used. For a small percentage of employees, the employee contributes the same amount for single and family coverage.

[2] The survey covers all 50 States and the District of Columbia. Collection was conducted between February and December 2000. The average reference period was July 2000.

[3] A classification system including about 480 individual occupations is used to cover all workers in the civilian economy. See the Technical Note for more information.

[4] A composite rate is a set contribution covering more than one benefit area, for example, health care and life insurance. Cost data for individual plans cannot be determined.

[5] Based on worker attributes. For example, employee contributions may vary based on earnings, length of service, or age.

[6] Amount varies by options selected under a "cafeteria plan" or employer-sponsored reimbursement account.

[7] Less than 0.5 percent.

NOTE: Because of rounding, sums of individual items may not equal totals. Where applicable, dash indicates no employees in this category.

**Table 6. Short-term disability:  Method of funding, full-time employees, private industry, National Compensation Survey, 2000**

| Type of funding | All employees | Professional, technical, and related employees | Blue-collar and service employees |
|---|---|---|---|
| Number (in thousands) with short-term disability ................ | 33,589 | 10,932 | 13,545 |
| | Percent | | |
| Total with short-term disability .. | 100 | 100 | 100 |
| Unfunded[1] ............................ | 10 | 12 | 4 |
| Insured ................................... | 30 | 30 | 32 |
| Self-insured ........................... | 36 | 34 | 38 |
| Legally required .................... | 14 | 12 | 14 |
| Unknown .............................. | 11 | 11 | 11 |
| Other ..................................... | ([2]) | ([2]) | 1 |

[1] Includes per disability sick leave plans, formerly reported under sick leave.

[2] Less than 0.5 percent.

NOTE:  Data were insufficient to show clerical and sales workers separately.  Because of rounding, sums of individual items may not equal totals. Where applicable, dash indicates no employees in this category, or data do not meet publication criteria.

# Chapter 2. Health Benefits

The National Compensation Survey collects information on a variety of health benefits, including medical, prescription drug, dental, and vision care. Definitions of major plan types, key provisions, and related terms follow.

## Medical Care

Medical care plans provide services or payments for services rendered in the hospital or by a physician. Those plans that provide only dental, vision, or prescription drug coverage are tabulated separately and described in their specific sections. Common plan types are fee-for-service plans, preferred provider organizations (PPOs), exclusive provider organizations (EPOs), and health maintenance organizations (HMOs).

### Health Care Plans and Systems

*Traditional fee-for-service plans: Indemnity and conventional indemnity plans.* A type of medical plan that reimburses the patient and/or provider as expenses are incurred and allows the participant the choice of any provider without effect on reimbursement.

*Preferred provider organization (PPO) plan.* An indemnity plan where coverage is provided to participants through a network of selected health care providers (such as hospitals and physicians). The enrollees may go outside the network, but would incur larger costs in the form of higher deductibles, higher coinsurance rates, or non-discounted charges from the providers.

*Exclusive provider organization (EPO) plan.* A more restrictive type of preferred provider organization plan under which employees must use providers from the specified network of physicians and hospitals to receive coverage; there is no coverage for care received from a non-network provider except in an emergency situation.

Note: The above three categories collectively are referred to as non-Health Maintenance Organizations or "non-HMOs" in a number of data tables.

**Health maintenance organization (HMO).** A health care system that assumes both the financial risks associated with providing comprehensive medical services (insurance and service risk) and the responsibility for health care delivery in a particular geographic area to HMO members, usually in return for a fixed, prepaid fee. Financial risk may be shared with the providers participating in the HMO.

*Group Model HMO.* An HMO that contracts with a single multi-specialty medical group to provide care to the HMO's membership. The group practice may work exclusively with the HMO, or it may provide services to non-HMO patients as well. The HMO pays the medical group a negotiated, per capita rate, which the group distributes among its physicians, usually on a salaried basis.

*Staff Model HMO.* A type of closed-panel HMO (where patients can receive services only through a limited number of providers) in which physicians are employees of the HMO. The physicians see patients in the HMO's own facilities.

*Network Model HMO.* An HMO model that contracts with multiple physician groups to provide services to HMO members; may involve large single and multi-specialty groups. The physician groups may provide services to both HMO and non-HMO plan participants.

*Individual Practice Association (IPA) HMO.* A type of health care provider organization composed of a group of independent practicing physicians who maintain their own offices and band together for the purpose of contracting their services to HMOs. An IPA may contract with and provide services to both HMO and non-HMO plan participants.

**Managed care plans.** Managed care plans generally provide comprehensive health services to their members, and offer financial incentives for patients to use the providers who belong to the plan. Examples of managed care plans include:

- Health maintenance organizations (HMOs),
- Preferred provider organizations (PPOs), and
- Exclusive provider organizations (EPOs).

*Managed care provisions.* Features within health plans that provide insurers with a way to manage the cost, use, and quality of health care services received by group members. Examples of managed care provisions include:

*Preadmission certification.* An authorization for hospital admission given by a health care provider to a group member prior to their hospitalization. Failure to obtain a pre-admission certification in non-emergency situations reduces or eliminates the health care provider's obligation to pay for services rendered.

*Utilization review.* The process of reviewing the appropriateness and quality of care provided to patients. Utilization review may take place before, during, or after the services are rendered.

*Preadmission testing.* A requirement designed to encourage patients to obtain necessary diagnostic services on an outpatient basis prior to non-emergency hospital admission. The testing is designed to reduce the length of a hospital stay.

*Non-emergency weekend admission restriction.* A requirement that imposes limits on reimbursement to patients for non-emergency weekend hospital admissions.

*Second surgical opinion.* A cost-management strategy that encourages or requires patients to obtain the opinion of another doctor after a physician has recommended that a non-emergency or elective surgery be performed. Programs may be voluntary or mandatory in that reimbursement is reduced or denied if the participant does not obtain the second opinion. Plans usually require that such opinions be obtained from board-certified specialists with no personal or financial interest in the outcome.

*Hospital audit program.* Some fee-for-service plans contain provisions that provide financial incentives for participants who uncover overcharges in their hospital bills.

## Limitations on coverage

*Maximum plan dollar limit.* The maximum amount payable by the insurer for covered expenses for the insured and each covered dependent while enrolled in the health plan.

- Plans can have a yearly and/or a lifetime maximum dollar limit.
- The most typical of maximums is a lifetime amount of $1 million per individual.

*Maximum out-of-pocket expense.* The maximum dollar amount a group member is required to pay out of pocket during a year. Until this maximum is met, the plan and group member shares in the cost of covered expenses. After the maximum is reached, the insurance carrier pays all covered expenses, often up to a lifetime maximum. (See previous definition.)

*Deductible.* A fixed dollar amount during the benefit period, usually a year, that an insured person pays before the insurer starts to make payments for covered medical services. Plans may have both individual and family deductibles.

- Some plans may have separate deductibles for specific services. For example, a plan may have a hospitalization deductible per admission.
- Deductibles may differ if services are received from an approved provider or if received from providers not on the approved list.

*Coinsurance.* A form of medical cost sharing in a health insurance plan that requires an insured person to pay a stated percentage of medical expenses after the deductible amount, if any, is paid.

- Once any deductible amount and coinsurance are paid, the insurer is responsible for the rest of the reimbursement for covered benefits up to allowed charges: the individual is responsible for any charges in excess of what the insurer determines to be "usual, customary and reasonable".
- Coinsurance rates may differ if services are received from an approved provider (i.e., a provider with whom the insurer has a contract or an agreement specifying payment levels and other contract requirements) or if received by providers not on the approved list.

*Multi-employer health plan.* Generally, an employee health benefit plan maintained pursuant to a collective bargaining agreement that includes employees of two or more employers. These plans are also known as Taft-Hartley plans or jointly administered plans. They are subject to federal but not State law (although States may regulate any insurance policies that they buy). They often self-insure.

*Premium.* Agreed-upon fees paid for coverage of medical benefits for a defined benefit period. Premiums can be paid by employers, unions, employees, or shared by both the insured individual and the plan sponsor.

*Self-insured plan.* A plan offered by employers who directly assume the major cost of health insurance for their employees. Some self-insured plans bear the entire risk. Other self-insured employers insure against large claims by purchasing stop-loss coverage. Some self-insured employers contract with insurance carriers or third party administrators for claims processing and other administrative services; other self-insured plans are self-administered. Minimum Premium Plans (MPP) are included in the self-insured health plan category. All types of plans can be financed on a self-insured basis.

*Stop-loss coverage.* A form of reinsurance for self-insured employers that limits the amount the employers will have to pay for each person's health care (individual limit) or for the total expenses of the employer (group limit).

### Alternatives to hospitalization

Alternatives to hospitalization are offered as a means of reducing costs.

*Extended care facilities.* These facilities provide skilled nursing care, rehabilitation, and convalescent services to patients who require less intensive treatment than that provided in a hospital.

*Home health care.* Such care programs provide skilled nursing and related services to patients in their own homes.

*Hospice care.* These services provide nursing care and psychological support to terminally ill patients and their families, either on an inpatient basis or in the patient's home.

### Mental health and substance abuse treatment

Mental health and substance abuse services include inpatient and outpatient care for psychiatric conditions and alcohol or drug dependency. The coverage for these conditions is generally more restrictive than that for general medical conditions.

*Detoxification.* This treatment involves supervised care by medical personnel designed to reduce or eliminate the symptoms of chemical dependency. Treatment can occur on an inpatient or outpatient basis.

*Rehabilitation services.* These services are intended to alter the behavior of substance abusers. They are usually provided after detoxification is complete. Treatment can occur on an inpatient or outpatient basis.

## Prescription Drugs

Prescription drug plans provide coverage for outpatient prescription drugs. Prescription drugs dispensed during a hospital stay are covered with hospital miscellaneous charges.

*Name brand drugs.* These are drugs that once were or still are under patents.

*Generic drugs.* Once a drug's patent has expired, some plans provide more generous coverage for same-formula generic drugs than for brand name drugs. Generic drugs are used as a cost-containment measure by some plans.

*Mail order drugs.* Used as a cost containment measure, some plans use mail order pharmacies that typically provide 3-month supplies of maintenance drugs.

## Dental Care

Dental care plans provide services or payments for preventive and restorative care and related dental services.

*Preventive services.* Such services include routine exams and x-rays.

*Restorative services.* These services include fillings, dental surgery, endodontics (root canal therapy), periodontics (treatment of gum disease), crowns, and prosthetics (replacement of missing teeth with bridgework or dentures).

*Orthodontia services.* Services for the correction of malpositioned teeth.

*Pretreatment authorization.* When a procedure is expected to exceed a certain cost, such as $300, pretreatment authorization must be obtained by the patient, usually from the dental claims administrator, before reimbursement will be made.

## Vision Care

Vision care plans provide coverage for eyeglasses, and with few exceptions, eye exams and contact lenses.

**Table 7. Medical care benefits: Coverage for selected services by type of plan, full-time employees, private industry, National Compensation Survey, 2000**

| Categories of care | All employees | | | Professional, technical, and related employees | | | Clerical and sales employees | | | Blue-collar and service employees | | |
|---|---|---|---|---|---|---|---|---|---|---|---|---|
| | All plans | Non-HMO plans | HMO plans | All plans | Non-HMO plans | HMO plans | All plans | Non-HMO plans | HMO plans | All plans | Non-HMO plans | HMO plans |
| Number of employees (in thousands) ......................... | 52,627 | 32,733 | 19,895 | 13,833 | 8,269 | 5,564 | 14,890 | 9,180 | 5,709 | 23,905 | 15,283 | 8,622 |
| | Percent | | | | | | | | | | | |
| Hospital room and board .......... | 100 | 100 | 100 | 100 | 100 | 100 | 100 | 100 | 100 | 100 | 100 | 100 |
| Inpatient surgery ...................... | 100 | 100 | 100 | 100 | 100 | 100 | 100 | 100 | 100 | 100 | 100 | 100 |
| Outpatient surgery[1] .................. | 100 | 100 | 100 | 100 | 100 | 100 | 100 | 100 | 100 | 100 | 100 | 100 |
| Inpatient physician visits ........... | 100 | 100 | 100 | 100 | 100 | 100 | 100 | 100 | 100 | 100 | 100 | 100 |
| Office physician visits .............. | 100 | 100 | 100 | 100 | 100 | 100 | 100 | 100 | 100 | 100 | 100 | 100 |
| Diagnostic X-ray and laboratory | 100 | 100 | 100 | 100 | 100 | 100 | 100 | 100 | 100 | 100 | 100 | 100 |
| Extended care[2] .......................... | 77 | 76 | 79 | 72 | 71 | 74 | 76 | 74 | 78 | 81 | 80 | 83 |
| Home health care[2] ..................... | 85 | 81 | 91 | 83 | 79 | 90 | 84 | 79 | 92 | 86 | 83 | 92 |
| Hospice care .......................... | 66 | 68 | 62 | 64 | 66 | 60 | 64 | 68 | 56 | 68 | 69 | 66 |
| Inpatient mental health ............ | 93 | 93 | 91 | 93 | 93 | 93 | 91 | 91 | 92 | 93 | 95 | 90 |
| Outpatient mental health .......... | 93 | 90 | 97 | 92 | 87 | 99 | 92 | 88 | 98 | 93 | 93 | 94 |
| Inpatient alcohol detoxification[3] | 94 | 92 | 98 | 95 | 92 | 99 | 94 | 91 | 99 | 95 | 93 | 97 |
| Inpatient alcohol rehabilitation[4] | 80 | 81 | 76 | 79 | 81 | 76 | 80 | 82 | 76 | 80 | 81 | 77 |
| Outpatient alcohol rehabilitation[4] ...................... | 85 | 84 | 87 | 85 | 81 | 90 | 84 | 82 | 87 | 86 | 87 | 86 |
| Inpatient drug detoxification[3] .... | 94 | 92 | 98 | 94 | 91 | 99 | 94 | 91 | 99 | 94 | 92 | 97 |
| Inpatient drug rehabilitation[4] ..... | 79 | 81 | 76 | 78 | 80 | 76 | 80 | 82 | 76 | 79 | 80 | 77 |
| Outpatient drug rehabilitation[4] .. | 84 | 83 | 87 | 84 | 80 | 90 | 83 | 81 | 87 | 85 | 85 | 84 |
| Hearing care[5] .......................... | 34 | 11 | - | 35 | 11 | - | 32 | 11 | - | 34 | 12 | - |
| Physical exam .......................... | 82 | 73 | 98 | 82 | 72 | 99 | 82 | 71 | 99 | 82 | 74 | 98 |
| Well-baby care ......................... | 84 | 76 | 97 | 86 | 78 | 98 | 84 | 77 | 96 | 83 | 76 | 97 |
| Immunization and inoculation ... | 61 | 47 | 84 | 64 | 49 | 88 | 61 | 45 | 86 | 59 | 48 | 80 |

[1] Charges incurred in the outpatient department of a hospital and outside the hospital.

[2] Some plans provide this care only to a patient who was previously hospitalized and is recovering without need of the extensive care provided by a general hospital.

[3] Detoxification is the systematic use of medication and other methods under medical supervision to reduce or eliminate the effects of substance abuse.

[4] Rehabilitation is designed to alter abusive behavior in patients once they are free of acute physical and mental complications.

[5] Plans provide, as a minimum, coverage for hearing examination expenses.

NOTE: Because of rounding, sums of individual items may not equal totals.
Where applicable, dash indicates no employees in this category, or data do not meet publication criteria.

**Table 8. Non-health maintenance organizations: Coverage for selected sevices, full-time employees, private industry, National Compensation Survey, 2000**

| Category of care and extent of coverage | All employees | Professional, technical, and related employees | Clerical and sales employees | Blue-collar and service employees |
|---|---|---|---|---|
| | Percent | | | |
| **Hospital room and board** | | | | |
| Total with coverage ................. | 100 | 100 | 100 | 100 |
| Covered in full ...................... | 6 | 7 | 11 | 3 |
| Subject to separate limits only[1] ............................... | 4 | 7 | 3 | 4 |
| Subject to separate limits plus major medical .......... | 13 | 19 | 11 | 10 |
| Major medical only[2] .............. | 77 | 66 | 75 | 83 |
| **Inpatient surgery** | | | | |
| Total with coverage ................. | 100 | 100 | 100 | 100 |
| Covered in full ...................... | 16 | 21 | 17 | 13 |
| Subject to separate limits only[1] ............................... | (3) | 1 | (3) | (3) |
| Subject to separate limits plus major medical .......... | 3 | 5 | 4 | 3 |
| Major medical only[2] .............. | 80 | 73 | 79 | 85 |
| **Outpatient surgery[4]** | | | | |
| Total with coverage ................. | 100 | 100 | 100 | 100 |
| Covered in full ...................... | 15 | 21 | 16 | 11 |
| Subject to separate limits only[1] ............................... | 2 | 2 | 1 | 2 |
| Subject to separate limits plus major medical .......... | 8 | 10 | 7 | 8 |
| Major medical only[2] .............. | 75 | 67 | 76 | 79 |
| **Inpatient physician visits** | | | | |
| Total with coverage ................. | 100 | 100 | 100 | 100 |
| Covered in full ...................... | 15 | 21 | 16 | 10 |
| Subject to separate limits only[1] ............................... | (3) | (3) | (3) | (3) |
| Subject to separate limits plus major medical .......... | 5 | 6 | 4 | 6 |
| Major medical only[2] .............. | 80 | 72 | 79 | 84 |

See footnotes at end of table.

**Table 8. Non-health maintenance organizations: Coverage for selected sevices, full-time employees, private industry, National Compensation Survey, 2000 — Continued**

| Category of care and extent of coverage | All employees | Professional, technical, and related employees | Clerical and sales employees | Blue-collar and service employees |
|---|---|---|---|---|
| | Percent | | | |
| **Office physician visits** | | | | |
| Total with coverage ................. | 100 | 100 | 100 | 100 |
| Subject to separate limits only[1] ............................... | 20 | 21 | 26 | 16 |
| Subject to separate limits plus major medical .......... | 42 | 41 | 40 | 45 |
| Major medical only[2] .............. | 38 | 38 | 34 | 39 |
| **Diagnostic x-ray and laboratory** | | | | |
| Total with coverage ................. | 100 | 100 | 100 | 100 |
| Covered in full ...................... | 15 | 21 | 16 | 12 |
| Subject to separate limits only[1] ............................... | 1 | 1 | 1 | (3) |
| Subject to separate limits plus major medical .......... | 6 | 4 | 7 | 6 |
| Major medical only[2] .............. | 78 | 74 | 76 | 82 |

[1] Separate limits apply to individual categories of care; e.g., separate limits or benefits for hospitalization. Limits may be set in terms of dollar or day ceilings on benefits, a requirement that the participant pay a percentage of costs (coinsurance), or a requirement that the participant pay a specific amount (deductible or copayment) before reimbursement begins or services are rendered.

[2] Major medical limits apply to all benefits under the plan, not selected individual benefits. Major medical limits are deductibles and coinsurance percentages that must be paid by the participant before any plan benefits begin, and overall limits on plan benefits that can be paid.

[3] Less than 0.5 percent.

[4] Charges incurred in the outpatient department of a hospital and outside of the hospital.

NOTE: Because of rounding, sums of individual items may not equal totals. Where applicable, dash indicates no employees in this category, or data do not meet publication criteria.

**Table 9. Non-health maintenance organizations: Coverage for alternatives to hospital care, full-time employees, private industry, National Compensation Survey, 2000**

| Category of care and extent of coverage | All em-ploy-ees | Profes-sional, techni-cal, and related em-ploy-ees | Clerical and sales em-ploy-ees | Blue-collar and service em-ploy-ees |
|---|---|---|---|---|
| | Percent | | | |
| **Extended care[1]** | | | | |
| Total with coverage ................. | 100 | 100 | 100 | 100 |
| Covered in full ...................... | 1 | 1 | 1 | 1 |
| Subject to separate limits only[2] ............................ | 14 | 20 | 18 | 10 |
| Subject to separate limits plus major medical ......... | 60 | 55 | 61 | 62 |
| Major medical only[3] ............. | 25 | 24 | 20 | 27 |
| **Home health care[1]** | | | | |
| Total with coverage ................. | 100 | 100 | 100 | 100 |
| Covered in full ...................... | 8 | 11 | 8 | 6 |
| Subject to separate limits only[2] ............................ | 9 | 13 | 11 | 6 |
| Subject to separate limits plus major medical ......... | 50 | 48 | 51 | 51 |
| Major medical only[3] ............. | 33 | 29 | 30 | 36 |
| **Hospice care** | | | | |
| Total with coverage ................. | 100 | 100 | 100 | 100 |
| Covered in full ...................... | 11 | 13 | 9 | 11 |
| Subject to separate limits only[2] ............................ | 7 | 8 | 11 | 3 |
| Subject to separate limits plus major medical ......... | 34 | 38 | 36 | 32 |
| Major medical only[3] ............. | 48 | 41 | 43 | 53 |

[1] Some plans provide this care only to a patient who was previously hospitalized and is recovering without need of the extensive care provided by a general hospital.

[2] Separate limits apply to individual categories of care; e.g., separate limits or benefits for extended care. Limits may be set in terms of dollar or day ceilings on benefits, a requirement that the participant pay a percentage of costs (coinsurance), or a requirement that the participant pay a specific amount (deductible or copayment) before reimbursement begins or services are rendered.

[3] Major medical limits apply to all benefits under the plan, not selected individual benefits. Major medical limits are deductibles and coinsurance percentages that must be paid by the participant before any plan benefits begin, and overall limits on plan benefits that can be paid.

NOTE: Because of rounding, sums of individual items may not equal totals. Where applicable, dash indicates no employees in this category, or data do not meet publication criteria.

**Table 10. Non-health maintenance organizations: Coverage for mental health and substance abuse, full-time employees, private industry, National Compensation Survey, 2000**

| Category of care and extent of coverage | All employees | Professional, technical, and related employees | Clerical and sales employees | Blue-collar and service employees |
|---|---|---|---|---|
| | Percent | | | |
| **Inpatient mental health** | | | | |
| Total with coverage ............... | 100 | 100 | 100 | 100 |
| Covered in full ...................... | 2 | 2 | 4 | 2 |
| Subject to separate limits only[1] ............................. | 10 | 12 | 15 | 7 |
| Subject to separate limits plus major medical .......... | 77 | 75 | 73 | 80 |
| Major medical only[2] ............. | 10 | 11 | 8 | 11 |
| **Outpatient mental health** | | | | |
| Total with coverage ............... | 100 | 100 | 100 | 100 |
| Covered in full ...................... | 1 | 1 | 1 | 1 |
| Subject to separate limits only[1] ............................. | 18 | 19 | 22 | 16 |
| Subject to separate limits plus major medical .......... | 80 | 80 | 76 | 83 |
| Major medical only[2] ............. | 1 | 1 | 1 | 1 |
| **Inpatient alcohol detoxification[3]** | | | | |
| Total with coverage ............... | 100 | 100 | 100 | 100 |
| Covered in full ...................... | 3 | 3 | 4 | 2 |
| Subject to separate limits only[1] ............................. | 10 | 12 | 14 | 7 |
| Subject to separate limits plus major medical .......... | 72 | 70 | 69 | 75 |
| Major medical only[2] ............. | 15 | 15 | 13 | 16 |
| **Inpatient alcohol rehabilitation[4]** | | | | |
| Total with coverage ............... | 100 | 100 | 100 | 100 |
| Covered in full ...................... | 2 | 1 | 4 | 2 |
| Subject to separate limits only[1] ............................. | 12 | 14 | 16 | 9 |
| Subject to separate limits plus major medical .......... | 82 | 82 | 77 | 85 |
| Major medical only[2] ............. | 3 | 3 | 3 | 4 |
| **Outpatient alcohol rehabilitation[4]** | | | | |
| Total with coverage ............... | 100 | 100 | 100 | 100 |
| Covered in full ...................... | ([5]) | 1 | 1 | - |
| Subject to separate limits only[1] ............................. | 17 | 19 | 23 | 12 |
| Subject to separate limits plus major medical .......... | 83 | 79 | 76 | 88 |
| Major medical only[2] ............. | ([5]) | 1 | ([5]) | ([5]) |

See footnotes at end of table.

**Table 10. Non-health maintenance organizations: Coverage for mental health and substance abuse, full-time employees, private industry, National Compensation Survey, 2000 — Continued**

| Category of care and extent of coverage | All employees | Professional, technical, and related employees | Clerical and sales employees | Blue-collar and service employees |
|---|---|---|---|---|
| | Percent | | | |
| **Inpatient drug detoxification[3]** | | | | |
| Total with coverage ............... | 100 | 100 | 100 | 100 |
| Covered in full ...................... | 3 | 3 | 4 | 2 |
| Subject to separate limits only[1] ............................. | 10 | 12 | 14 | 7 |
| Subject to separate limits plus major medical .......... | 72 | 71 | 69 | 75 |
| Major medical only[2] ............. | 15 | 15 | 13 | 16 |
| **Inpatient drug rehabilitation[4]** | | | | |
| Total with coverage ............... | 100 | 100 | 100 | 100 |
| Covered in full ...................... | 2 | 1 | 4 | 2 |
| Subject to separate limits only[1] ............................. | 12 | 13 | 16 | 9 |
| Subject to separate limits plus major medical .......... | 82 | 82 | 77 | 86 |
| Major medical only[2] ............. | 3 | 3 | 3 | 4 |
| **Outpatient drug rehabilitation[4]** | | | | |
| Total with coverage ............... | 100 | 100 | 100 | 100 |
| Covered in full ...................... | ([5]) | 1 | 1 | - |
| Subject to separate limits only[1] ............................. | 16 | 19 | 23 | 11 |
| Subject to separate limits plus major medical .......... | 83 | 80 | 76 | 89 |
| Major medical only[2] ............. | ([5]) | 1 | ([5]) | ([5]) |

[1] Separate limits apply to individual categories of care; e.g., separate limits or benefits for inpatient mental health. Limits may be set in terms of dollar or day ceilings on benefits, a requirement that the participant pay a percentage of costs (coinsurance), or a requirement that the participant pay a specific amount (deductible or copayment) before reimbursement begins or services are rendered.

[2] Major medical limits apply to all benefits under the plan, not selected individual benefits. Major medical limits are deductibles and coinsurance percentages that must be paid by the participant before any plan benefits begin, and overall limits on plan benefits that can be paid.

[3] Detoxification is the systematic use of medication and other methods under medical supervision to reduce or eliminate the effects of substance abuse.

[4] Rehabilitation is designed to alter abusive behavior in patients once they are free of acute physical and mental complications.

[5] Less than 0.5 percent.

NOTE: Because of rounding, sums of individual items may not equal totals. Where applicable, dash indicates no employees in this category, or data do not meet publication criteria.

**Table 11. Health maintenance organizations: Coverage for selected services, full-time employees, private industry, National Compensation Survey, 2000**

| Category of care and extent of coverage | All employees | Professional, technical, and related employees | Clerical and sales employees | Blue-collar and service employees |
|---|---|---|---|---|
| | Percent | | | |
| **Hospital room and board** | | | | |
| Total with coverage .................. | 100 | 100 | 100 | 100 |
| Covered in full ........................ | 59 | 56 | 60 | 59 |
| Subject to limits[1] .................... | 41 | 44 | 40 | 41 |
| **Inpatient surgery** | | | | |
| Total with coverage .................. | 100 | 100 | 100 | 100 |
| Covered in full ........................ | 84 | 88 | 84 | 80 |
| Subject to limits[1] .................... | 16 | 12 | 16 | 20 |
| **Outpatient surgery[2]** | | | | |
| Total with coverage .................. | 100 | 100 | 100 | 100 |
| Covered in full ........................ | 67 | 72 | 72 | 60 |
| Subject to limits[1] .................... | 33 | 28 | 28 | 40 |
| **Inpatient physician visits** | | | | |
| Total with coverage .................. | 100 | 100 | 100 | 100 |
| Covered in full ........................ | 85 | 89 | 85 | 82 |
| Subject to limits[1] .................... | 15 | 11 | 15 | 18 |
| **Office physician visits** | | | | |
| Total with coverage .................. | 100 | 100 | 100 | 100 |
| Covered in full ........................ | 7 | 9 | 4 | 7 |
| Subject to limits[1] .................... | 93 | 91 | 96 | 93 |
| **Diagnostic x-ray and laboratory services** | | | | |
| Total with coverage .................. | 100 | 100 | 100 | 100 |
| Covered in full ........................ | 81 | 83 | 80 | 80 |
| Subject to limits[1] .................... | 19 | 17 | 20 | 20 |

[1] Limits may be set in terms of dollar or day ceilings on benefits, a requirement that the participant pay a percentage of costs (coinsurance), or a requirement that the participant pay a specific amount (deductible or copayment) before reimbursement begins or services are rendered.
[2] Charges incurred in the outpatient department of a hospital and outside of the hospital.

NOTE: Because of rounding, sums of individual items may not equal totals. Where applicable, dash indicates no employees in this category, or data do not meet publication criteria.

**Table 12. Health maintenance organizations: Coverage for alternatives to hospital care, full-time employees, private industry, National Compensation Survey, 2000**

| Category of care and extent of coverage | All employees | Professional, technical, and related employees | Clerical and sales employees | Blue-collar and service employees |
|---|---|---|---|---|
| | Percent | | | |
| **Extended care[1]** | | | | |
| Total with coverage .................. | 100 | 100 | 100 | 100 |
| Covered in full ........................ | 15 | 18 | 14 | 14 |
| Subject to limits[2] .................... | 85 | 82 | 86 | 86 |
| **Home health care[1]** | | | | |
| Total with coverage .................. | 100 | 100 | 100 | 100 |
| Covered in full ........................ | 66 | 71 | 71 | 61 |
| Subject to limits[2] .................... | 34 | 29 | 29 | 39 |
| **Hospice care** | | | | |
| Total with coverage .................. | 100 | 100 | 100 | 100 |
| Covered in full ........................ | 52 | 50 | 44 | 58 |
| Subject to limits[2] .................... | 48 | 50 | 56 | 42 |

[1] Some plans provide this care only to a patient who was previously hospitalized and is recovering without need of the extensive care provided by a general hospital.
[2] Limits may be set in terms of dollar or day ceilings on benefits, a requirement that the participant pay a percentage of cost (coinsurance), or a requirement that the participant pay a specific amount (deductible or copayment) before reimbursement begins or services are rendered.

NOTE: Because of rounding, sums of individual items may not equal totals. Where applicable, dash indicates no employees in this category, or data do not meet publication criteria.

**Table 13. Health maintenance organizations: Coverage for mental health and substance abuse treatment, full-time employees, private industry, National Compensation Survey, 2000**

| Category of care and extent of coverage | All employees | Professional, technical, and related employees | Clerical and sales employees | Blue-collar and service employees |
|---|---|---|---|---|
| | Percent | | | |
| **Inpatient mental health** | | | | |
| Total with coverage .................. | 100 | 100 | 100 | 100 |
| Covered in full ...................... | 10 | 11 | 7 | 12 |
| Subject to limits[1] .................. | 90 | 89 | 93 | 88 |
| **Outpatient mental health** | | | | |
| Total with coverage .................. | 100 | 100 | 100 | 100 |
| Covered in full ...................... | 3 | 3 | 1 | 3 |
| Subject to limits[1] .................. | 97 | 97 | 99 | 97 |
| **Inpatient alcohol detoxification[2]** | | | | |
| Total with coverage .................. | 100 | 100 | 100 | 100 |
| Covered in full ...................... | 24 | 21 | 25 | 25 |
| Subject to limits[1] .................. | 76 | 79 | 75 | 75 |
| **Inpatient alcohol rehabilitation[3]** | | | | |
| Total with coverage .................. | 100 | 100 | 100 | 100 |
| Covered in full ...................... | 7 | 10 | 8 | 5 |
| Subject to limits[1] .................. | 93 | 90 | 92 | 95 |
| **Outpatient alcohol rehabilitation[3]** | | | | |
| Total with coverage .................. | 100 | 100 | 100 | 100 |
| Covered in full ...................... | ([4]) | ([4]) | ([4]) | ([4]) |
| Subject to limits[1] .................. | 100 | 100 | 100 | 100 |

See footnotes at end of table.

**Table 13. Health maintenance organizations: Coverage for mental health and substance abuse treatment, full-time employees, private industry, National Compensation Survey, 2000 — Continued**

| Category of care and extent of coverage | All employees | Professional, technical, and related employees | Clerical and sales employees | Blue-collar and service employees |
|---|---|---|---|---|
| | Percent | | | |
| **Inpatient drug detoxification[2]** | | | | |
| Total with coverage .................. | 100 | 100 | 100 | 100 |
| Covered in full ...................... | 24 | 21 | 25 | 25 |
| Subject to limits[1] .................. | 76 | 79 | 75 | 75 |
| **Inpatient drug rehabilitation[3]** | | | | |
| Total with coverage .................. | 100 | 100 | 100 | 100 |
| Covered in full ...................... | 7 | 10 | 8 | 5 |
| Subject to limits[1] .................. | 93 | 90 | 92 | 95 |
| **Outpatient drug rehabilitation[3]** | | | | |
| Total with coverage .................. | 100 | 100 | 100 | 100 |
| Covered in full ...................... | ([4]) | ([4]) | ([4]) | ([4]) |
| Subject to limits[1] .................. | 100 | 100 | 100 | 100 |

[1] Limits may be set in terms of dollar or day ceilings on benefits, a requirement that the participant pay a percentage of cost (coinsurance), or a requirement that the participant pay a specific amount (deductible or copayment) before reimbursement begins or services are rendered.
[2] Detoxification is the systematic use of medication and other methods under medical supervision to reduce or eliminate the effects of substance abuse.
[3] Rehabilitation is designed to alter abusive behavior in patients once they are free of acute physical and mental complications.
[4] Less than 0.5 percent.

NOTE: Because of rounding, sums of individual items may not equal totals. Where applicable, dash indicates no employees in this category, or data do not meet publication criteria.

**Table 14.  Medical care benefits:[1]  Fee arrangement and financial intermediary, full-time employees, private industry, National Compensation Survey, 2000**

| Fee arrangement | All employees | Professional, technical, and related employees | Clerical and sales employees | Blue-collar and service employees |
|---|---|---|---|---|
| Number (in thousands) with medical care ...................... | 52,627 | 13,833 | 14,890 | 23,905 |
| | Percent | | | |
| Total with medical care ............. | 100 | 100 | 100 | 100 |
| Traditional fee-for-service[2] ... | 9 | 9 | 9 | 8 |
| Self insured[3] ....................... | 4 | 6 | 5 | 3 |
| With administrative services contract[4] ... | 3 | 3 | 3 | 2 |
| Without administrative services contract ..... | (5) | 1 | 1 | (5) |
| Not determinable .......... | 1 | 2 | 2 | 1 |
| Fully insured ...................... | 4 | 3 | 4 | 5 |
| Combined financing .......... | (5) | (5) | - | - |
| Preferred provider organization[6] ................... | 51 | 49 | 50 | 53 |
| Self insured[3] ....................... | 30 | 32 | 25 | 32 |
| With administrative services contract[4] ... | 22 | 24 | 18 | 24 |
| Without administrative services contract ..... | 3 | 3 | 2 | 4 |
| Not determinable .......... | 5 | 5 | 5 | 4 |
| Fully insured ...................... | 19 | 15 | 22 | 20 |
| Combined financing .... | 2 | 1 | 3 | 1 |

See footnotes at end of table.

**Table 14.  Medical care benefits:[1]  Fee arrangement and financial intermediary, full-time employees, private industry, National Compensation Survey, 2000 — Continued**

| Fee arrangement | All employees | Professional, technical, and related employees | Clerical and sales employees | Blue-collar and service employees |
|---|---|---|---|---|
| | Percent | | | |
| Total with medical care | | | | |
| Health maintenance organization[7] .................. | 38 | 40 | 38 | 36 |
| Self insured[3] ..................... | 5 | 6 | 5 | 4 |
| Fully insured ..................... | 33 | 34 | 33 | 32 |
| Other[8] ................................. | 2 | 2 | 2 | 2 |

[1] Plans providing services or payments for services rendered in the hospital or by a physician.  Excludes plans that provided only dental, vision, or prescription drug coverage.

[2] These plans pay for specific medical procedures as expenses are incurred.

[3] Includes plans that are financed on a pay-as-you-go basis, plans financed through contributions to a trust fund established to pay benefits, and plans operating their own facilities if at least partially financed by employer contributions.  Includes plans that are administered by a commercial carrier through Administrative Services Only (ASO) contracts.

[4] An arrangement where an establishment pays the cost of benefits, but hires another establishment to handle administrative services.

[5] Less than 0.5 percent.

[6] A preferred provider organization (PPO) is a group of hospitals and physicians that contracts to provide comprehensive medical services.  To encourage use by organization members, the health care plan limits reimbursement rates when participants use nonmember services.

[7] Delivers comprehensive health care on a prepayment rather than fee-for-service basis.

[8] Includes exclusive provider organizations, which are groups of hospitals and physicians that contract to provide comprehensive medical services. Participants are required to obtain services from members of the organization in order to receive plan benefits.

NOTE:  Because of rounding, sums of individual items may not equal totals. Where applicable, dash indicates no employees in this category, or data do not meet publication criteria.

**Table 15. Health maintenance organizations: Summary of selected features, full-time employees, private industry, National Compensation Survey, 2000**

| Selected features | All employees | Professional, technical, and related employees | Clerical and sales employees | Blue-collar and service employees |
|---|---|---|---|---|
| Number (in thousands) in HMO plans ................................. | 19,895 | 5,564 | 5,709 | 8,622 |
| | Percent | | | |
| Total in HMO plans ................... | 100 | 100 | 100 | 100 |
| Model type: | | | | |
| Group/staff[1] ...................... | 14 | 13 | 11 | 16 |
| Individual practice association[2] ............... | 38 | 42 | 39 | 35 |
| Mixed model ...................... | 26 | 25 | 31 | 22 |
| Not determinable .............. | 23 | 20 | 19 | 27 |
| Point of service feature[3] ....... | 44 | 46 | 45 | 41 |
| Limit on copayments[4] .......... | 30 | 31 | 29 | 29 |
| Preventive dental care[5] ........ | 12 | 13 | 17 | 9 |

[1] Care is provided at centralized locations.
[2] Care is provided by doctors working out of their offices.
[3] Enrollees may obtain care from non-HMO providers, with limited reimbursement.
[4] In these plans, HMOs limit the dollar amount the individual pays, after which coverage is in full. For example, there is a copayment limit of $1,000 after which the HMO covers all services at 100 percent.
[5] Includes dental examinations and/or x-rays only.

NOTE: Because of rounding, sums of individual items may not equal totals. Where applicable, dash indicates no employees in this category, or data do not meet publication criteria.

**Table 16. Non-health maintenance organizations: Amount and type of individual deductible,[1] full-time employees, private industry, National Compensation Survey, 2000**

| Deductible[2] | All employees | | | Professional, technical, and related employees | | | Clerical and sales employees | | | Blue-collar and service employees | | |
|---|---|---|---|---|---|---|---|---|---|---|---|---|
| | All non-HMO plans[3] | Fee-for-service plans | Pre-ferred pro-vider organi-zations | All non-HMO plans[3] | Fee-for-service plans | Pre-ferred pro-vider organi-zations | All non-HMO plans[3] | Fee-for-service plans | Pre-ferred pro-vider organi-zations | All non-HMO plans[3] | Fee-for-service plans | Pre-ferred pro-vider organi-zations |
| Number (in thousands) in non-HMO plans ................. | 32,733 | 4,593 | 26,959 | 8,269 | 1,222 | 6,740 | 9,180 | 1,374 | 7,440 | 15,283 | 1,997 | 12,779 |
| | Percent | | | | | | | | | | | |
| Total in non-HMO plans ........... | 100 | 100 | 100 | 100 | 100 | 100 | 100 | 100 | 100 | 100 | 100 | 100 |
| Deductible specified ............. | 72 | 94 | 70 | 65 | 94 | 63 | 70 | 98 | 67 | 78 | 92 | 76 |
| Deductible on an annual basis[4] ......................... | 72 | 94 | 70 | 65 | 94 | 63 | 69 | 98 | 66 | 77 | 92 | 76 |
| Based on earnings[5] ...... | 1 | 3 | 1 | 2 | 1 | 2 | 1 | 2 | 1 | 1 | 4 | (6) |
| Flat dollar amount ......... | 71 | 91 | 69 | 63 | 93 | 61 | 68 | 96 | 66 | 76 | 87 | 75 |
| Less than $100 ......... | 1 | 4 | (6) | 1 | 5 | (6) | (6) | (6) | (6) | 1 | 5 | (6) |
| $100 ........................ | 5 | 8 | 5 | 4 | 8 | 3 | 5 | 8 | 5 | 6 | 8 | 6 |
| $101 - $149 ............. | (6) | 3 | (6) | (6) | 1 | (6) | (6) | 3 | - | (6) | 4 | (6) |
| $150 ........................ | 2 | 2 | 1 | 1 | 2 | 1 | 1 | 1 | 1 | 4 | 2 | 2 |
| $151 - $199 ............. | (6) | - | (6) | - | - | - | (6) | - | (6) | (0) | - | (6) |
| $200 ........................ | 17 | 25 | 16 | 20 | 40 | 17 | 14 | 32 | 11 | 16 | 11 | 18 |
| $201 - $249 ............. | (6) | - | 1 | 1 | - | 2 | - | - | - | (6) | - | (6) |
| $250 ........................ | 16 | 28 | 14 | 12 | 19 | 11 | 16 | 29 | 15 | 17 | 33 | 15 |
| $251 - $299 ............. | - | - | - | - | - | - | - | - | - | - | - | - |
| $300 ........................ | 9 | 6 | 11 | 6 | 4 | 6 | 10 | 3 | 12 | 11 | 7 | 12 |
| Over $300 ................. | 20 | 17 | 21 | 19 | 15 | 21 | 20 | 19 | 21 | 20 | 18 | 21 |
| Other ............................. | 1 | - | 1 | (6) | - | (6) | 1 | - | 1 | 1 | - | 1 |
| No deductible ..................... | 28 | 5 | 29 | 35 | 6 | 37 | 30 | 2 | 33 | 22 | 6 | 24 |
| Not determinable ................. | (6) | 1 | (6) | (6) | (6) | - | (6) | (6) | (6) | (6) | 2 | (6) |
| | Average[7] | | | | | | | | | | | |
| Average annual deductible ....... | $334 | $362 | $331 | $336 | $344 | $333 | $345 | $370 | $340 | $328 | $366 | $326 |

[1] The deductible is the amount of covered expenses that an individual must pay before any charges are paid by the medical care plan. Deductibles that apply separately to a specific category of expense, such as a deductible for each hospital admission, were excluded from this tabulation.

[2] Amount of deductible described is for each insured person. However, many plans contain a maximum family deductible. In some plans, the individual and the family deductibles are identical. If the deductible applied only to dependents' coverage, it was not tabulated.

[3] These plans include fee-for-service, preferred provider organizations, and exclusive provider organizations. Data are not shown separately for exclusive provider organizations.

[4] Deductibles are calculated on an annual basis, with the enrollee responsible for satisfying a new deductible requirement each plan year.

[5] These plans have deductibles that vary by the amount of the participant's earnings.

[6] Less than 0.5 percent.

[7] The average is presented for all covered workers; averages exclude workers without the plan provision.

NOTE: Because of rounding, sums of individual items may not equal totals. Where applicable, dash indicates no employees in this category, or data do not meet publication criteria

21

**Table 17. Non-health maintenance organizations: Relationship of individual and family deductibles,[1] full-time employees, private industry, National Compensation Survey, 2000**

| Relationship of individual and family deductibles | All employees | | | Professional, technical, and related employees | | | Clerical and sales employees | | | Blue-collar and service employees | | |
|---|---|---|---|---|---|---|---|---|---|---|---|---|
| | All non-HMO plans[2] | Fee-for-service plans | Pre-ferred pro-vider organi-zations | All non-HMO plans[2] | Fee-for-service plans | Pre-ferred pro-vider organi-zations | All non-HMO plans[2] | Fee-for-service plans | Pre-ferred pro-vider organi-zations | All non-HMO plans[2] | Fee-for-service plans | Pre-ferred pro-vider organi-zations |
| Number (in thousands) in non-HMO plans ................. | 32,733 | 4,593 | 26,959 | 8,269 | 1,222 | 6,740 | 9,180 | 1,374 | 7,440 | 15,283 | 1,997 | 12,779 |
| | Percent | | | | | | | | | | | |
| Total with non-HMO plans ........ | 100 | 100 | 100 | 100 | 100 | 100 | 100 | 100 | 100 | 100 | 100 | 100 |
| Individual and family deductibles specified ...... | 65 | 74 | 65 | 60 | 82 | 59 | 62 | 87 | 60 | 70 | 61 | 72 |
| Family deductible is multiple of individual deductible[3] .................. | 61 | 72 | 61 | 56 | 78 | 55 | 58 | 84 | 56 | 66 | 60 | 67 |
| 2 times ......................... | 31 | 43 | 28 | 32 | 39 | 32 | 31 | 50 | 28 | 30 | 41 | 27 |
| 2.5 times ...................... | 2 | - | 2 | 2 | - | 2 | 1 | - | 2 | 2 | - | 2 |
| 3 times ......................... | 26 | 20 | 29 | 20 | 28 | 20 | 24 | 23 | 25 | 31 | 14 | 35 |
| Specified number of individual deductibles must be met to satisfy family deductible[4] ....... | 4 | 2 | 4 | 4 | 4 | 4 | 3 | 3 | 4 | 5 | 1 | 5 |
| Less than 3 individual deductibles ............. | 1 | 2 | 1 | 1 | 3 | 1 | 1 | 3 | 1 | 2 | (5) | 2 |
| 3 individual deductibles | 3 | 1 | 3 | 3 | 1 | 3 | 3 | 1 | 3 | 3 | (5) | 3 |
| More than 3 individual deductibles ............. | - | - | - | - | - | - | - | - | - | - | - | - |
| No individual and/or family deductible ........................ | 34 | 24 | 34 | 40 | 17 | 41 | 38 | 12 | 40 | 29 | 37 | 27 |
| Not determinable ................. | (5) | 1 | (5) | (5) | (5) | - | (5) | (5) | (5) | (5) | 2 | (5) |

[1] Deductibles are calculated on an annual basis with the enrollee responsible for satisfying a new deductible requirement each plan year.

[2] These plans include fee-for-service, preferred provider organizations, and exclusive provider organizations. Data are not shown separately for exclusive provider organizations.

[3] For example, the individual deductible requirement is $100 while the family deductible requirement is $300. Includes some multiples not shown separately.

[4] For example, the individual requirement is $100 and three individual deductibles must be met to satisfy the family requirement.

[5] Less than 0.5 percent.

NOTE: Because of rounding, sums of individual items may not equal totals. Where applicable, dash indicates no employees in this category, or data do not meet publication criteria.

**Table 18. Non-health maintenance organizations: Coinsurance rates, full-time employees, private industry, National Compensation Survey, 2000**

| Coinsurance | All employees | | | Professional, technical, and related employees | | | Clerical and sales employees | | | Blue-collar and service employees | | |
|---|---|---|---|---|---|---|---|---|---|---|---|---|
| | All non-HMO plans[1] | Fee-for-service plans | Preferred provider organizations | All non-HMO plans[1] | Fee-for-service plans | Preferred provider organizations | All non-HMO plans[1] | Fee-for-service plans | Preferred provider organizations | All non-HMO plans[1] | Fee-for-service plans | Preferred provider organizations |
| Number (in thousands) in non-HMO plans ............ | 32,733 | 4,593 | 26,959 | 8,269 | 1,222 | 6,740 | 9,180 | 1,374 | 7,440 | 15,283 | 1,997 | 12,779 |
| | Percent | | | | | | | | | | | |
| Total with non-HMO plans ........ | 100 | 100 | 100 | 100 | 100 | 100 | 100 | 100 | 100 | 100 | 100 | 100 |
| With coinsurance[2] ............... | 76 | 92 | 74 | 69 | 97 | 67 | 74 | 89 | 73 | 80 | 90 | 79 |
| Coinsurance rate[3] | | | | | | | | | | | | |
| 80 percent ..................... | 40 | 76 | 35 | 39 | 87 | 32 | 42 | 69 | 39 | 39 | 74 | 35 |
| 85 percent ..................... | 4 | 1 | 3 | 2 | ([4]) | 2 | 3 | ([4]) | 3 | 5 | 2 | 4 |
| 90 percent ..................... | 30 | 8 | 35 | 28 | 7 | 32 | 25 | 7 | 30 | 34 | 10 | 39 |
| Other percent ............... | 2 | 7 | 1 | 1 | 3 | ([4]) | 3 | 14 | 1 | 2 | 4 | 1 |
| Without coinsurance[5] ........... | 24 | 8 | 26 | 31 | 3 | 33 | 26 | 11 | 27 | 20 | 10 | 21 |

[1] These plans include fee-for-service, preferred provider organizations, and exclusive provider organizations. Data are not shown separately for exclusive provider organizations.

[2] Represents the initial coinsurance in plans that have 100 percent coverage after the individual pays a specified dollar amount toward expenses. For example, the plan pays 80 percent until the individual's out-of-pocket expenses reach $1,000, and then coverage is at 100 percent.

[3] A few plans have more than one coinsurance rate. In those cases, the coinsurance rate shown is that which applies to the majority of benefits under the plan. Includes variable coinsurance rates not shown separately.

[4] Less than 0.5 percent.

[5] Includes plans with overall benefit limitations, such as maximum dollar amounts and deductibles, where the coinsurance rate is 100 percent.

NOTE: Because of rounding, sums of individual items may not equal totals. Where applicable, dash indicates no employees in this category, or data do not meet publication criteria.

**Table 19. Non-health maintenance organizations: Maximum out-of-pocket expense provisions, full-time employees, private industry, National Compensation Survey, 2000**

| Type and amount of out-of-pocket expense provision | All employees | | Professional, technical, and related employees | | Clerical and sales employees | | Blue-collar and service employees | |
|---|---|---|---|---|---|---|---|---|
| | All non-HMO plans[1] | Pre-ferred pro-vider organi-zations | All non-HMO plans[1] | Pre-ferred pro-vider organi-zations | All non-HMO plans[1] | Pre-ferred pro-vider organi-zations | All non-HMO plans[1] | Pre-ferred pro-vider organi-zations |
| Number (in thousands) with non-HMO plans ................. | 32,733 | 26,959 | 8,269 | 6,740 | 9,180 | 7,440 | 15,283 | 12,779 |
| | Percent | | | | | | | |
| Total with non-HMO plans ........ | 100 | 100 | 100 | 100 | 100 | 100 | 100 | 100 |
| With limit on out-of-pocket expense ......................... | 80 | 81 | 77 | 78 | 78 | 79 | 83 | 84 |
| With an annual dollar maximum on out-of-pocket expense[2] ..................... | 77 | 77 | 75 | 76 | 73 | 73 | 80 | 80 |
| Per individual: | | | | | | | | |
| Less than $400 ......... | 3 | 3 | 4 | 3 | 4 | 3 | 2 | 2 |
| $400 ...................... | 3 | 2 | 2 | 2 | 3 | 3 | 3 | 2 |
| $401 - $400 .......... | 1 | 1 | 2 | 2 | - | - | (3) | (3) |
| $500 ...................... | 6 | 7 | 7 | 8 | 6 | 7 | 6 | 6 |
| $501 - $999 .............. | 11 | 9 | 11 | 9 | 9 | 5 | 13 | 12 |
| $1000 ...................... | 15 | 15 | 12 | 12 | 14 | 14 | 18 | 17 |
| $1,001 - $1,499 ........ | 6 | 7 | 7 | 8 | 4 | 5 | 6 | 8 |
| $1,500 ...................... | 10 | 10 | 12 | 14 | 11 | 12 | 7 | 8 |
| $1,501 - $1,999 ........ | 4 | 4 | 3 | 3 | 5 | 6 | 4 | 4 |
| $2,000 ...................... | 8 | 8 | 7 | 8 | 8 | 7 | 9 | 9 |
| Greater than $2,000 | 10 | 10 | 7 | 7 | 10 | 10 | 12 | 12 |
| Per family: | | | | | | | | |
| Less than $1,000 ...... | 5 | 4 | 7 | 6 | 5 | 4 | 3 | 3 |
| $1,000 ...................... | 4 | 5 | 6 | 6 | 3 | 4 | 4 | 4 |
| $1,001 - $1,999 ........ | 9 | 8 | 11 | 10 | 9 | 7 | 8 | 8 |
| $2,000 ...................... | 8 | 5 | 8 | 6 | 7 | 5 | 9 | 5 |
| $2,001 - $2,999 ........ | 5 | 6 | 5 | 6 | 3 | 3 | 6 | 8 |
| $3,000 ...................... | 9 | 10 | 5 | 6 | 8 | 9 | 12 | 13 |
| Greater than $3,000 | 23 | 25 | 23 | 26 | 23 | 26 | 22 | 24 |
| No family maximum .. | 9 | 9 | 6 | 5 | 9 | 10 | 10 | 10 |
| Family maximum cannot be computed[4] .......... | 5 | 5 | 4 | 5 | 4 | 4 | 6 | 5 |
| Annual maximum on out-of-pocket expense based on earnings ...... | (3) | 1 | (3) | (3) | 1 | 1 | (3) | (3) |
| Annual maximum on out-of-pocket expense varies by coinsurance rate[5] ........................... | 3 | 3 | 2 | 2 | 4 | 5 | 2 | 3 |
| Other ................................. | (3) | (3) | - | - | - | - | (3) | (3) |
| No out-of-pocket expense required[6] ........................ | 10 | 10 | 13 | 12 | 13 | 13 | 7 | 7 |
| No limit on out-of-pocket expense .......................... | 8 | 7 | 9 | 8 | 7 | 7 | 8 | 8 |
| Not determinable .................. | 2 | 2 | 2 | 2 | 1 | 1 | 2 | 2 |

See footnotes at end of table.

**Table 19. Non-health maintenance organizations: Maximum out-of-pocket expense provisions, full-time employees, private industry, National Compensation Survey, 2000 — Continued**

| Type and amount of out-of-pocket expense provision | All employees | | Professional, technical, and related employees | | Clerical and sales employees | | Blue-collar and service employees | |
|---|---|---|---|---|---|---|---|---|
| | All non-HMO plans[1] | Pre-ferred pro-vider organi-zations | All non-HMO plans[1] | Pre-ferred pro-vider organi-zations | All non-HMO plans[1] | Pre-ferred pro-vider organi-zations | All non-HMO plans[1] | Pre-ferred pro-vider organi-zations |
| | Average[7] | | | | | | | |
| Average annual dollar maximum on individual out-of-pocket expense ........ | $1,469 | $1,506 | $1,254 | $1,260 | $1,476 | $1,526 | $1,574 | $1,618 |
| Average annual dollar maximum on family out-of-pocket expense ........ | 3,165 | 3,297 | 2,787 | 2,869 | 3,329 | 3,542 | 3,278 | 3,398 |

[1] These plans include fee-for-service, preferred provider organizations, and exclusive provider organizations. Data are not shown separately for fee-for-service or exclusive provider organizations.

[2] Deductible amounts were excluded from computation of the out-of-pocket dollar limits. With rare exceptions, an out-of-pocket limit was specified on an annual basis. Few workers were in plans where the expense limit applied to a disability or a period other than a year. Charges for certain services, such as mental health care, may not be counted toward the out-of-pocket maximum.

[3] Less than 0.5 percent.

[4] These are plans where a family maximum is stated in such a way that it cannot be computed. For example, the individual out-of-pocket expense is limited to $1,000 per year, and the family out-of-pocket expense is limited to three individuals. The family out-of-pocket expense cannot be computed because each of the three individuals must separately reach an out-of-pocket limit of $1,000. Thus, if two individuals each reach $1,000 in their out-of-pocket expenses, and two other family members reach $900 and $800 respectively in out-of-pocket expenses, the family out-of-pocket limit would not have been met. A family dollar maximum cannot be computed in this example.

[5] Some plans reimburse medical expenses at more than one coinsurance rate. They impose a limit on out-of-pocket expenses by specifying a maximum on covered medical expenses beyond which all expenses are paid at 100 percent.

[6] All covered expenses are paid at 100 percent.

[7] The average is presented for all covered workers; averages exclude workers without the plan provision.

NOTE: Because of rounding, sums of individual items may not equal totals. Where applicable, dash indicates no employees in this category, or data do not meet publication criteria.

**Table 20. Non-health maintenance organizations:  Maximum benefit provisions, full-time employees, private industry, National Compensation Survey, 2000**

| Maximum[1] | All employees | Profes-sional, techni-cal, and related em-ploy-ees | Clerical and sales em-ploy-ees | Blue-collar and service employees |
|---|---|---|---|---|
| Number (in thousands) with non-HMO plans .................. | 32,733 | 8,269 | 9,180 | 15,283 |
| Percent | | | | |
| Total with non-HMO plans ........ | 100 | 100 | 100 | 100 |
| With maximum limits ............. | 63 | 60 | 58 | 67 |
| Lifetime maximum only[2] ... | 61 | 60 | 57 | 65 |
| Under $500,000 ........... | 1 | 1 | ( [3] ) | 2 |
| $500,000 ...................... | 1 | 1 | 1 | 2 |
| $1,000,000 .................. | 32 | 27 | 32 | 36 |
| $1,500,000 .................. | 4 | 6 | 4 | 3 |
| $2,000,000 .................. | 13 | 16 | 11 | 14 |
| More than $2,000,000 .. | 7 | 4 | 10 | 7 |
| Annual or disability maximum only ............ | 1 | 1 | 1 | 2 |
| Both lifetime and annual or disability maximums ... | ( [3] ) | ( [3] ) | - | ( [3] ) |
| Other maximum ............... | ( [3] ) | - | - | ( [3] ) |
| Without maximum limits ........ | 33 | 35 | 36 | 30 |
| Not determinable .................. | 4 | 4 | 6 | 3 |
| Average[4] | | | | |
| Average lifetime maximum ....... | $1,657,680 | $1,529,649 | $1,828,424 | $1,630,773 |

[1]  Maximum described is for each insured person.  Where the maximum differed for employees and dependents, the employee maximum was tabulated.
[2]  Includes other lifetime maximum limits not shown separately.
[3]  Less than 0.5 percent.
[4]  The average is presented for all covered workers; averages exclude workers without the plan provision.

NOTE:   Because of rounding, sums of individual items may not equal totals.   Where applicable, dash indicates no employees in this category, or data do not meet publication criteria.

**Table 21. Non-health maintenance organizations: Average major medical provisions, full-time employees, private industry, National Compensation Survey, 2000**

| Average[1] | All employees | Profes-sional, technical, and related employees | Clerical and sales employees | Blue-collar and service employees |
|---|---|---|---|---|
| Annual deductible[2] | | | | |
| Individual ............................... | $334 | $336 | $345 | $328 |
| Family ................................... | 799 | 793 | 848 | 776 |
| Annual out-of-pocket expense maximum[3] | | | | |
| Individual ............................... | 1,469 | 1,254 | 1,476 | 1,574 |
| Family ................................... | 3,165 | 2,787 | 3,329 | 3,278 |
| Lifetime maximum[4] ................... | 1,657,680 | 1,529,649 | 1,828,424 | 1,630,773 |

[1] The average is presented for all covered workers; averages exclude workers without the plan provision.

[2] The deductible is the amount of covered expenses that an individual or family must pay before any charges are paid by the medical care plan. Deductibles that apply separately to a specific category of expense, such as a deductible for each hospital admission, were excluded from this tabulation.

[3] The out-of-pocket expense maximum is the amount an individual or family must pay before the plan will pay 100 percent of additional charges. Deductible amounts were excluded from computation of the out-of-pocket dollar limits. Usually, out-of-pocket limits were specified on an annual basis. Charges for certain services, such as mental health care, may not be counted toward the out-of-pocket maximum.

[4] The maximum is the total amount of expenses that the plan will pay. Maximum described is for each insured person. Where the maximum differed for employees and dependents, the employee maximum was tabulated.

NOTE: Where applicable, dash indicates no employees in this category, or data do not meet publication criteria.

**Table 22. Preferred provider organizations:[1] Summary of selected features, full-time employees, private industry, National Compensation Survey, 2000**

| Type of services and incentives | All employees | Professional, technical, and related employees | Clerical and sales employees | Blue-collar and service employees |
|---|---|---|---|---|
| Number (in thousands) in PPO plans ............................ | 26,959 | 6,740 | 7,440 | 12,779 |
| | Percent | | | |
| Total with PPO plans ................ | 100 | 100 | 100 | 100 |
| Services subject to PPO incentive: | | | | |
| Hospital room and board .. | 93 | 92 | 93 | 93 |
| Surgery ............................ | 94 | 96 | 94 | 92 |
| Physician's in-hospital visits ............................ | 94 | 96 | 94 | 92 |
| Office visits ...................... | 92 | 96 | 90 | 91 |
| Outpatient prescription drugs ............................ | 37 | 43 | 35 | 35 |
| Type of PPO incentive:[2] | | | | |
| Coinsurance rate differs ... | 91 | 91 | 90 | 91 |
| Lower annual deductible ... | 58 | 60 | 57 | 57 |
| Higher lifetime maximum benefit limit ................. | 10 | 12 | 9 | 8 |
| Lower catastrophic maximum limit ............. | 70 | 77 | 68 | 68 |
| Lower hospital deductible .. | 18 | 17 | 19 | 19 |
| Office visits copayment ..... | 65 | 66 | 66 | 64 |
| Outpatient prescription drugs copayment ........ | 18 | 21 | 16 | 17 |
| Discounted for PPO[3] ........ | 30 | 31 | 28 | 30 |
| Not determinable .............. | 4 | 3 | 5 | 5 |

[1] A preferred provider organization (PPO) is a group of hospitals and physicians that contract to provide comprehensive medical services. To encourage use by organization members, the health care plan limits reimbursement rates when participants use nonmember services.

[2] Sum of individual items is greater than the total because many plan participants were in plans with more than one incentive.

[3] The amount of total expenses incurred by the individual is discounted under the PPO. For example, under the non-PPO, total expenses are $10,000; under the PPO, total expenses are discounted by 10 percent.

NOTE: Because of rounding, sums of individual items may not equal totals. Where applicable, dash indicates no employees in this category, or data do note meet publication criteria.

**Table 23. Preferred provider organizations:[1] Coinsurance rate for preferred service providers versus other service providers, full-time employees, private industry, National Compensation Survey, 2000**

| Coinsurance rate comparison | All employees | Professional, technical, and related employees | Clerical and sales employees | Blue-collar and service employees |
|---|---|---|---|---|
| Number (in thousands) in PPO plans ................................. | 26,959 | 6,740 | 7,440 | 12,779 |
| | Percent | | | |
| Total with PPO plans ................ | 100 | 100 | 100 | 100 |
| Overall coinsurance rate differs ............................. | 91 | 91 | 90 | 91 |
| 100 vs 80 ........................... | 14 | 16 | 16 | 13 |
| 90 vs 80 ............................. | 8 | 12 | 7 | 7 |
| 100 vs 70 ........................... | 5 | 9 | 6 | 3 |
| 90 vs 70 ............................. | 22 | 16 | 22 | 25 |
| 80 vs 70 ............................. | 5 | 2 | 7 | 5 |
| 80 vs 60 ............................. | 17 | 11 | 18 | 20 |
| 80 vs 50 ............................. | 4 | 7 | 4 | 3 |
| Other coinsurance rate ..... | 15 | 17 | 12 | 16 |
| Overall coinsurance rate does not differ ................. | 8 | 8 | 8 | 8 |
| Not determinable ................. | 2 | 1 | 3 | 1 |

[1] A preferred provider organization (PPO) is a group of hospitals and physicians that contract to provide comprehensive medical services. To encourage use by organization members, the health care plan limits reimbursement rates when participants use nonmember services.

NOTE: Because of rounding, sums of individual items may not equal totals. Where applicable, dash indicates no employees in this category, or data do not meet publication criteria.

**Table 24. Medical care benefits: Availability of managed care benefits, full-time employees, private industry, National Compensation Survey, 2000**

| Managed care plan | All employees | Professional, technical, and related employees | Clerical and sales employees | Blue-collar and service employees |
|---|---|---|---|---|
| Number (in thousands) with medical care ...................... | 52,627 | 13,833 | 14,890 | 23,905 |
| | Percent | | | |
| Total with medical care ............. | 100 | 100 | 100 | 100 |
| With managed care benefits | 96 | 97 | 97 | 95 |
| Traditional fee-for-service with managed care features[1] ...................... | 5 | 6 | 6 | 3 |
| Preferred provider organization[2] ............... | 51 | 49 | 50 | 53 |
| Exclusive provider organization[3] ............... | 2 | 2 | 2 | 2 |
| Prepaid health maintenance organization[4] ............... | 38 | 40 | 38 | 36 |
| Without managed care ......... | 3 | 2 | 3 | 4 |
| Not determinable .................. | 1 | 1 | 1 | 1 |

[1] Fee-for-service plans with preadmission certification or mandatory second surgical opinion features.

[2] A preferred provider organization (PPO) is a group of hospitals and physicians that contract to provide comprehensive medical services. To encourage use by organization members, the health care plan limits reimbursement rates when participants use nonmember services.

[3] An exclusive provider organization is a group of hospitals and physicians that contract to provide comprehensive medical services. Participants are required to obtain services from members of the organization to receive plan benefits.

[4] A health maintenance organization provides a prescribed set of benefits to enrollees for a fixed payment.

NOTE: Because of rounding, sums of individual items may not equal totals. Where applicable, dash indicates no employees in this category, or data do not meet publication criteria.

**Table 25. Non-health maintenance organizations: Availability of selected cost containment features, full-time employees, private industry, National Compensation Survey, 2000**

| Cost containment features | All employees | Professional, technical, and related employees | Clerical and sales employees | Blue-collar and service employees |
|---|---|---|---|---|
| Number (in thousands) in non-HMO plans .................. | 32,733 | 8,269 | 9,180 | 15,283 |
| | Percent | | | |
| Total with non-HMO plans ........ | 100 | 100 | 100 | 100 |
| With cost containment features ............................ | 72 | 67 | 68 | 77 |
| Preadmission certification requirement ................ | 63 | 60 | 62 | 64 |
| Utilization or concurrent review .................... | 39 | 36 | 36 | 43 |
| Preadmission testing ........ | 26 | 23 | 20 | 30 |
| Nonemergency weekend admission restriction ... | 9 | 7 | 7 | 11 |
| Hospital audit program ..... | 5 | 3 | 3 | 7 |
| Without cost containment feature ......................... | 25 | 28 | 29 | 20 |
| Data not available ................ | 3 | 5 | 3 | 3 |

NOTE: Sum of individual items may be greater than the total because many participants were in plans with more than one type of cost containment feature. Where applicable, dash indicates no employees in this category, or data do not meet publication criteria.

**Table 26. Non-health maintenance organizations: Prehospitalization certification requirements, full-time employees, private industry, National Compensation Survey, 2000**

| Preadmission requirements | All employees | Professional, technical, and related employees | Clerical and sales employees | Blue-collar and service employees |
|---|---|---|---|---|
| Number (in thousands) with preadmission certification ... | 20,483 | 4,929 | 5,702 | 9,851 |
| | Percent | | | |
| Total with preadmission certification ......................... | 100 | 100 | 100 | 100 |
| Plan does not impose penalty ........................... | 6 | 4 | 7 | 7 |
| Plan does impose penalty .... | 94 | 96 | 93 | 93 |
| No benefit ........................... | 5 | 7 | 3 | 5 |
| Deductible on hospital admission ..................... | 45 | 47 | 45 | 43 |
| Less than $200 ............. | 4 | 7 | 3 | 3 |
| $200 - $299 .................. | 13 | 10 | 17 | 12 |
| $300 - $399 .................. | 4 | 3 | 3 | 5 |
| $400 - $499 .................. | 3 | 4 | 4 | 1 |
| $500 or greater ............. | 21 | 24 | 19 | 21 |
| Reduced coinsurance ....... | 24 | 25 | 23 | 24 |
| Without a maximum dollar penalty .......... | 17 | 18 | 16 | 18 |
| With a maximum dollar penalty .................... | 6 | 7 | 6 | 7 |
| Reduced coinsurance and separate deductible per admission ............. | (1) | (1) | (1) | (1) |
| Other ................................. | 2 | 2 | 1 | 3 |
| Penalty not determinable .. | 18 | 15 | 21 | 18 |

[1] Less than 0.5 percent.

NOTE: Because of rounding, sums of individual items may not equal totals. Where applicable, dash indicates no employees in this category, or data do not meet publication criteria.

**Table 27. Non-health maintenance organizaiotns: Second surgical opinion provisions, full-time employees, private industry, National Compensation Survey, 2000**

| Second surgical opinion requirements | All employees | Professional, technical, and related employees | Clerical and sales employees | Blue-collar and service employees |
|---|---|---|---|---|
| Number (in thousands) in non-HMO plans .................. | 32,733 | 8,269 | 9,180 | 15,283 |
| | Percent | | | |
| Total with non-HMO plans ........ | 100 | 100 | 100 | 100 |
| With second surgical opinion program ......................... | 44 | 45 | 34 | 49 |
| With no penalties for non-compliance .......... | 34 | 38 | 24 | 37 |
| With penalties for non-compliance .......... | 10 | 7 | 9 | 12 |
| No second surgical opinion program[1] ..................... | 52 | 47 | 62 | 48 |
| Not determinable ................. | 5 | 9 | 4 | 3 |

[1] Includes plans in which documentation does not detail a second surgical opinion program. By definition, managed care plans, such as preferred provider organizations, integrate second surgical opinion programs as part of their structure. These managed care plans are quite often responsible for initiating the second surgical opinion program. When this occurs, that program was not tabulated.

NOTE: Because of rounding, sums of individual items may not equal totals. Where applicable, dash indicates no empoyees in this category, or data do not meet publication criteria.

**Table 28. Health maintenance organization: Hospital room and board coverage copayment provisions,[1] full-time employees, private industry, National Compensation Survey, 2000**

| Type of copayment provision | All employees | Professional, technical, and related employees | Clerical and sales employees | Blue-collar and service employees |
|---|---|---|---|---|
| Number (in thousands) with separate copayment ........... | 5,349 | 1,701 | 1,489 | 2,160 |
| | Percent | | | |
| Total with separate copayment | 100 | 100 | 100 | 100 |
| Per confinement ................... | 79 | 83 | 72 | 80 |
| $50 ............................ | 1 | 1 | 1 | 1 |
| $100 .......................... | 23 | 28 | 29 | 14 |
| $150 .......................... | 1 | 1 | 3 | - |
| $200 .......................... | 6 | 8 | 8 | 3 |
| $250 .......................... | 16 | 20 | 9 | 17 |
| $300 .......................... | 4 | ([2]) | 4 | 6 |
| $400 .......................... | 4 | - | 1 | 9 |
| $500 .......................... | 14 | 15 | 6 | 19 |
| Greater than $500 ........... | ([2]) | 1 | - | ([2]) |
| Other ......................... | 10 | 8 | 12 | 11 |
| Limited to maximum amount per year[3] ...................... | 10 | 4 | 9 | 15 |
| Copayment per year ............. | 2 | 3 | ([2]) | 2 |
| Copayment per day ............. | 21 | 17 | 27 | 20 |

[1] A copayment is the amount of covered expenses that an individual must pay before any charges are paid by the medical care plan.
[2] Less than 0.5 percent.
[3] Limits placed on the maximum copayment an individual pays during the year. For example, an individual is subject to a copayment of $100 per confinement with a limit of $300 per year.

NOTE: Because of rounding, sums of individual items may not equal totals. Where applicable, dash indicates no employees in this category, or data do not meet publication criteria.

**Table 29. Non-health maintenance organizations: Types of limitations on extended care facilities, full-time employees, private industry, National Compensation Survey, 2000**

| Type of limit | All employees | Professional, technical, and related employees | Clerical and sales employees | Blue-collar and service employees |
|---|---|---|---|---|
| Number (in thousands) in non-HMO plans with extended care benefits ....... | 24,866 | 5,857 | 6,835 | 12,174 |
| | Percent | | | |
| Total in non-HMO plans with extended care benefits ....... | 100 | 100 | 100 | 100 |
| Covered in full ....................... | 1 | 1 | 1 | 1 |
| Subject to limits other than major medical[1] ............... | 75 | 75 | 79 | 72 |
| Limit on days ................... | 67 | 67 | 73 | 64 |
| Limit on dollars ............... | 7 | 4 | 6 | 10 |
| Separate coinsurance ....... | 9 | 7 | 7 | 10 |
| Limited to maximum percentage rate of prior hospital confinement ............... | 7 | 8 | 7 | 7 |
| Other limits ..................... | 2 | 3 | 1 | 1 |
| Major medical limits only ...... | 25 | 24 | 20 | 27 |

[1] Major medical limits apply to all benefits under the plan, not selected individual benefits. Major medical limits are deductibles and coinsurance percentages that must be paid by the participant before any plan benefits begin, and overall limits on plan benefits that can be paid.

NOTE: Sum of individual items is greater than the total because some participants were in plans with more than one type of limit. Where applicable, dash indicates no employees in this category, or data do not meet publication criteria.

**Table 30.  Non-health maintenance organizations:  Limitations on days of extended care facilities coverage, full-time employees, private industry, National Compensation Survey, 2000**

| Day limits | All employees | Professional, technical, and related employees | Clerical and sales employees | Blue-collar and service employees |
|---|---|---|---|---|
| Number (in thousands) in non-HMO plans with day limits on extended care ....... | 16,715 | 3,939 | 4,980 | 7,795 |
| | Percent | | | |
| Total in non-HMO plans with day limits on extended care | 100 | 100 | 100 | 100 |
| First dollar coverage[1] for a limited number of days per confinement .............. | 5 | 2 | 4 | 6 |
| Major medical coverage[2] for a limited number of days per confinement ............. | 19 | 23 | 17 | 18 |
| First dollar coverage[1] for a limited number of days per year ........................ | 23 | 34 | 28 | 15 |
| Major medical coverage[2] for a limited number of days per year ........................ | 52 | 39 | 49 | 61 |
| 60 days ............................. | 15 | 16 | 16 | 15 |
| 90 days ............................. | 3 | 2 | 4 | 3 |
| 100 days ........................... | 11 | 7 | 10 | 13 |
| 120 days ........................... | 13 | 10 | 14 | 14 |
| Other ................................. | 10 | 4 | 4 | 16 |
| First dollar coverage[1] for a limited number of days per lifetime ...................... | ([3]) | 1 | ([3]) | - |
| Major medical coverage[2] for a limited number of days per lifetime ...................... | 1 | 1 | 2 | ([3]) |

[1] Includes plans in which all expenses were reimbursed for the full semiprivate room rate, up to a specified dollar amount.
[2] Major medical limits apply to all benefits under the plan, not selected individual benefits.  Major medical limits are deductibles and coinsurance percentages that must be paid by the participant before any plan benefits begin, and overall limits on plan benefits that can be paid.
[3] Less than 0.5 percent.

NOTE:  Because of rounding, sums of individual items may not equal totals. Where applicable, dash indicates no empoyees in this category, or data do not meet publication criteria.

**Table 31.  Health maintenance organizations:  Extent of coverage for extended care facilities, full-time employees, private industry, National Compensation Survey, 2000**

| Type of coverage | All employees | Professional, technical, and related employees | Clerical and sales employees | Blue-collar and service employees |
|---|---|---|---|---|
| Number (in thousands) in HMO plans with extended care benefits ..................... | 15,744 | 4,119 | 4,455 | 7,170 |
| | Percent | | | |
| Total in HMO plans with extended care benefits ....... | 100 | 100 | 100 | 100 |
| Covered in full ........................ | 15 | 18 | 14 | 14 |
| Day limit ................................. | 71 | 63 | 68 | 77 |
| Per year[1] ......................... | 56 | 52 | 50 | 62 |
| 100 days ........................ | 26 | 25 | 25 | 28 |
| Per confinement ............... | 15 | 11 | 18 | 15 |
| Per lifetime ...................... | ([2]) | ([2]) | ([2]) | ([2]) |
| A limit other than a day limit applies ........... | 14 | 19 | 18 | 9 |

[1] Other day limit periods are not shown separately.
[2] Less than 0.5 percent.

NOTE:  Because of rounding, sums of individual items may not equal totals. Where applicable, dash indicates no employees in this category, or data do not meet publication criteria.

**Table 32. Non-health maintenance organizations: Extent of coverage for surgical services, full-time employees, private industry, National Compensation Survey, 2000**

| Type of surgery and extent of coverage | All employees | Professional, technical, and related employees | Clerical and sales employees | Blue-collar and service employees |
|---|---|---|---|---|
| Number (in thousands) in non-HMO plans with inpatient surgery ................. | 32,733 | 8,269 | 9,180 | 15,283 |
| Number (in thousands) in non-HMO plans with outpatient surgery ............... | 32,733 | 8,269 | 9,180 | 15,283 |
| Percent | | | | |
| **Inpatient surgery** | | | | |
| Total in non-HMO plans with inpatient surgery ............. | 100 | 100 | 100 | 100 |
| Covered in full ................... | 16 | 21 | 17 | 13 |
| Subject to limits other than major medical ............. | 4 | 6 | 4 | 3 |
| Dollar limit ...................... | 1 | (1) | 2 | 1 |
| Separate coinsurance ... | 1 | 2 | 1 | 1 |
| Separate deductible ...... | 1 | 1 | (1) | 1 |
| Other limit ...................... | 1 | 2 | 1 | (1) |
| Major medical limits only[2] | 80 | 73 | 79 | 85 |
| **Outpatient surgery**[3] | | | | |
| Total in non-HMO plans with outpatient surgery ........... | 100 | 100 | 100 | 100 |
| Covered in full ................... | 15 | 21 | 16 | 11 |
| Subject to limits other than major medical ............. | 10 | 12 | 8 | 10 |
| Dollar limit ...................... | 1 | (1) | 2 | 1 |
| Separate coinsurance ... | 2 | 2 | 1 | 3 |
| Separate deductible ...... | 6 | 7 | 4 | 6 |
| Other limit ...................... | 1 | 3 | 1 | (1) |
| Major medical limits only[2] | 75 | 67 | 76 | 79 |

[1] Less than 0.5 percent.
[2] Major medical limits apply to all benefits under the plan, not selected individual benefits. Major medical limits are deductibles and coinsurance percentages that must be paid by the participant before any plan benefits begin, and overall limits on plan benefits that can be paid.
[3] Charges incurred in the outpatient department of a hospital and outside of the hospital.

NOTE: Sum of individual items is greater than the total because some participants were in plans with more than one type of limit. Where applicable, dash indicates no employees in this category, or data do not meet publication criteria.

**Table 33. Health maintenance organizations: Extent of coverage for physician's office visits, full-time employees, private industry, National Compensation Survey, 2000**

| Type of coverage | All employees | Professional, technical, and related employees | Clerical and sales employees | Blue-collar and service employees |
|---|---|---|---|---|
| Number (in thousands) in HMO plans with physician's office visits coverage ................... | 19,895 | 5,564 | 5,709 | 8,622 |
| Percent | | | | |
| Total in HMO plans with physician's office visits coverage ........................... | 100 | 100 | 100 | 100 |
| Covered in full ...................... | 7 | 9 | 4 | 7 |
| Subject to a copayment[1] ...... | 92 | 90 | 95 | 91 |
| Less than $5 ................... | 4 | 7 | 5 | 3 |
| $5 ................................. | 11 | 12 | 11 | 11 |
| $10 ................................ | 47 | 42 | 52 | 46 |
| $15 ................................ | 23 | 23 | 23 | 24 |
| More than $15 ............... | 5 | 4 | 4 | 7 |
| Unspecified copayment .... | (2) | (2) | (2) | - |
| Subject to other limits only .... | 1 | 1 | 1 | 2 |
| Not determinable ................. | (2) | (2) | (2) | (2) |

[1] Includes other copayments not shown seperately.
[2] Less than 0.5 percent.

NOTE: Because of rounding, sums of individual items may not equal totals. Where applicable, dash indicates no employees in this category, or data do not meet publication criteria.

**Table 34. Outpatient prescription drug benefits: Summary of coverage, full-time employees, private industry, National Compensation Survey, 2000**

| Selected features | All employees | Professional, technical, and related employees | Clerical and sales employees | Blue-collar and service employees |
|---|---|---|---|---|
| Number of employees (in thousands) with outpatient prescription drug coverage | 50,464 | 13,380 | 14,112 | 22,972 |
| | Percent | | | |
| Total with outpatient prescription drug coverage | 100 | 100 | 100 | 100 |
| Coverage for brand name drugs | 99 | 99 | 99 | 99 |
| Higher reimbursement for generic drugs | 78 | 78 | 84 | 74 |
| Coverage for mail order drugs[1] | 64 | 64 | 64 | 65 |
| Higher reimbursement for prescriptions filled at selected pharmacies | 42 | 45 | 39 | 42 |

[1] Programs that provide drugs for maintenance purposes, that is, drugs required on a continuous basis.

NOTE: Sum of individual items is greater than the total because some participants were in plans with more than one type of coverage. Where applicable, dash indicates no employees in this category, or data do not meet publication criteria.

**Table 35. Outpatient prescription drug benefits: Brand name drug provisions in non-health maintenance organizations, full-time employees, private industry, National Compensation Survey, 2000**

| Type of coverage | All employees | Professional, technical, and related employees | Clerical and sales employees | Blue-collar and service employees |
|---|---|---|---|---|
| Number of employees (in thousands) in non-HMO plans with outpatient brand name drug coverage | 31,304 | 8,024 | 8,540 | 14,739 |
| | Percent | | | |
| Total in non-HMO plans with outpatient brand name drug coverage | 100 | 100 | 100 | 100 |
| Covered in full | ([1]) | ([1]) | ([1]) | - |
| Covered with limits: | | | | |
| Subject to the major medical limits of plan | 59 | 58 | 54 | 63 |
| Subject to copayment per prescription[2] | 57 | 53 | 63 | 56 |
| Less than $10.00 | 7 | 6 | 4 | 10 |
| $10.00 | 13 | 15 | 16 | 9 |
| $15.00 | 18 | 15 | 22 | 18 |
| More than $15.00 | 14 | 10 | 17 | 14 |
| Unspecified copayment | 2 | 1 | ([1]) | 3 |
| Subject to a separate yearly deductible | 7 | 9 | 8 | 6 |
| Subject to a separate coinsurance rate | 9 | 8 | 8 | 10 |
| Subject to a separate yearly maximum | 4 | ([1]) | 4 | 5 |
| Difference in cost between generic and brand name drugs[3] | 15 | 15 | 14 | 15 |
| Other | 4 | 8 | 4 | 3 |
| Not determinable | 4 | 4 | 4 | 4 |

[1] Less than 0.5 percent.
[2] Includes copayment amounts not shown separately.
[3] In these plans, the participant is required to use a generic equivalent when available; if a generic equivalent is not chosen, the individual must pay the difference in total cost between the brand name and generic drug plus any required copayment. For example, if an individual is subject to a $5 copayment for generic drugs and the brand name equivalent is purchased, the individual must pay the difference in total cost between the brand name and generic drug, plus the $5 copayment.

NOTE: Sum of individual items is greater than the total because some participants were in plans with more than one type of coverage. Where applicable, dash indicates no employees in this category, or data do not meet publication criteria.

**Table 36. Outpatient prescription drug benefits: Brand name drug provisions in health maintenance organizations, full-time employees, private industry, National Compensation Survey, 2000**

| Type of coverage | All employees | Professional, technical, and related employees | Clerical and sales employees | Blue-collar and service employees |
|---|---|---|---|---|
| Number of employees (in thousands) in HMO plans with outpatient brand name drug coverage .................... | 18,611 | 5,207 | 5,490 | 7,913 |
| | Percent | | | |
| Total in HMO plans with outpatient brand name drug coverage .............. | 100 | 100 | 100 | 100 |
| Covered in full .......................... | (1) | (1) | (1) | (1) |
| Covered with limits: | | | | |
| Subject to copayment per prescription[2] .................. | 68 | 73 | 73 | 62 |
| Less than $10.00 .... | 6 | 8 | 5 | 5 |
| $10.00 ............................. | 26 | 27 | 30 | 23 |
| $15.00 ............................. | 20 | 23 | 23 | 15 |
| $20.00 ............................. | 7 | 7 | 5 | 8 |
| More than $20.00 ............ | (1) | - | (1) | (1) |
| Unspecified copayment .... | 8 | 3 | 4 | 8 |
| Subject to a separate yearly deductible ..................... | 4 | 4 | 0 | 3 |
| Subject to a separate yearly maximum ......................... | 2 | 1 | 2 | 3 |
| Difference in cost between generic and brand name drugs[3] ............................. | 20 | 19 | 21 | 19 |
| Other ....................................... | 8 | 8 | 7 | 10 |
| Not determinable .................. | 6 | 3 | 2 | 10 |

[1] Less than 0.5 percent.
[2] Includes copayment amounts not shown separately.
[3] In these plans, the participant is required to use a generic equivalent when available; if a generic equivalent is not chosen, the individual must pay the difference in total cost between the brand name and generic drug plus any required copayment. For example, if an individual is subject to a $5 copayment for generic drugs and the brand name equivalent is purchased, the individual must pay the difference in total cost between the brand name and generic drug, plus the $5 copayment.

NOTE: Sum of individual items is greater than the total because some participants were in plans with more than one type of coverage. Where applicable, dash indicates no employees in this category, or data do not meet publication criteria.

**Table 37. Mental health care benefits: Comparison of coverage for hospital room and board and outpatient care with other illnesses, full-time employees, private industry, National Compensation Survey, 2000**

| Relationship to coverage for other illnesses | All employees | Professional, technical, and related employees | Clerical and sales employees | Blue-collar and service employees |
|---|---|---|---|---|
| | Percent | | | |
| **Inpatient care** | | | | |
| Total covered ...................... | 100 | 100 | 100 | 100 |
| Covered the same ................... | 13 | 13 | 11 | 14 |
| Covered differently .................. | 87 | 87 | 89 | 86 |
| **Outpatient care[1]** | | | | |
| Total covered ...................... | 100 | 100 | 100 | 100 |
| Covered the same ................... | 6 | 7 | 4 | 7 |
| Covered differently .................. | 94 | 93 | 96 | 93 |

[1] Includes treatment in one or more of the following: outpatient department of a hospital, residential treatment center, organized outpatient clinic, day-night treatment center, or doctor's office. If benefits differed by location of treatment, the location offering the most beneficial coverage was tabulated.

NOTE: Because of rounding, sums of individual items may not equal totals. Where applicable, dash indicates no employees in this category, or data do not meet publication criteria.

**Table 38. Mental health care benefits: Separate limits on coverage, full-time employees, private industry, National Compensation Survey, 2000**

| Coverage limitation | All employees | Professional, technical, and related employees | Clerical and sales employees | Blue-collar and service employees |
|---|---|---|---|---|
| Number (in thousands) with inpatient mental health care benefits ............... | 48,739 | 12,866 | 13,564 | 22,309 |
| Number (in thousands) with outpatient mental health care benefits ............ | 48,712 | 12,691 | 13,710 | 22,311 |
| | Percent | | | |
| **Inpatient care** | | | | |
| Total with mental health care benefits ............ | 100 | 100 | 100 | 100 |
| No separate limits[1] ........... | 15 | 15 | 13 | 15 |
| Subject to separate limits[2] | 85 | 85 | 87 | 85 |
| Days ............... | 76 | 72 | 77 | 77 |
| Dollars ............ | 10 | 9 | 9 | 10 |
| Coinsurance ............... | 13 | 11 | 15 | 13 |
| Copayment ............... | 3 | 4 | 4 | 3 |
| Other[3] ............ | 4 | 5 | 5 | 3 |
| **Outpatient care[4]** | | | | |
| Total with mental health care benefits ............ | 100 | 100 | 100 | 100 |
| No separate limits[1] ........... | 7 | 8 | 5 | 9 |
| Subject to separate limits[2] | 93 | 92 | 95 | 91 |
| Days ............... | 72 | 74 | 75 | 70 |
| Dollars ............ | 15 | 15 | 10 | 17 |
| Coinsurance ............... | 20 | 16 | 21 | 21 |
| Copayment ............... | 30 | 35 | 32 | 25 |
| Other[3] ............ | 16 | 10 | 20 | 17 |

**Table 39. Mental health care benefits: Separate limits on coverage in health maintenance organizations, full-time employees, private industry, National Compensation Survey, 2000**

| Coverage limitation | All employees | Professional, technical, and related employees | Clerical and sales employees | Blue-collar and service employees |
|---|---|---|---|---|
| Number (in thousands) with inpatient mental health care benefits ............... | 18,171 | 5,189 | 5,229 | 7,752 |
| Number (in thousands) with outpatient mental health care benefits ............ | 19,206 | 5,499 | 5,610 | 8,098 |
| | Percent | | | |
| **Inpatient care** | | | | |
| Total with mental health care benefits ............ | 100 | 100 | 100 | 100 |
| No separate limits[1] ........... | 15 | 16 | 11 | 16 |
| Subject to separate limits[2] | 85 | 84 | 89 | 84 |
| Days ............... | 77 | 73 | 81 | 77 |
| Dollars ............ | 7 | 5 | 7 | 8 |
| Coinsurance ............... | 10 | 0 | 16 | 9 |
| Copayment ............... | 5 | 6 | 5 | 4 |
| Other[3] ............ | 2 | 3 | 2 | 2 |
| **Outpatient care[4]** | | | | |
| Total with mental health care benefits ............ | 100 | 100 | 100 | 100 |
| No separate limits[1] ........... | 9 | 11 | 5 | 10 |
| Subject to separate limits[2] | 91 | 89 | 95 | 90 |
| Days ............... | 77 | 74 | 81 | 75 |
| Dollars ............ | 8 | 6 | 5 | 12 |
| Coinsurance ............... | 6 | 5 | 9 | 5 |
| Copayment ............... | 44 | 48 | 47 | 39 |
| Other[3] ............ | 8 | 7 | 11 | 7 |

[1] These include plans that provide coverage without any separate limits; they also include plans that provide coverage subject to only the major medical limits of the plan.
[2] Separate limitations indicate that mental health care benefits are more restrictive than benefits for other treatments. For example, if a plan limits inpatient mental health care to 30 days per year, that plan contains separate limits. The total is less than the sum of the individual items because many plans had more than one type of limitation.
[3] These are plans when comparisons were made between copayments and coinsurances for mental health care and all other illnesses. For example, outpatient mental health care had a 50 percent coinsurance payment while office visits for other illnesses had a $10 copayment.
[4] Includes treatment in one or more of the following: outpatient department of a hospital, residential treatment center, organized outpatient clinic, day-night treatment center, or doctor's office. If benefits differed by location of treatment, doctor's office care was tabulated.

NOTE: Sum of individual items is greater than total because some participants were in plans with more than one type of limit. Where applicable, dash indicates no employees in this category, or data do not meet publication criteria.

[1] These include plans that provide coverage without any separate limits; they also include plans that provide coverage subject to only the major medical limits of the plan.
[2] Separate limitations indicate that mental health care benefits are more restrictive than benefits for other treatments. For example, if a plan limits inpatient mental health care to 30 days per year, that plan contains separate limits. The total is less than the sum of the individual items because many plans had more than one type of limitation.
[3] These are plans when comparisons were made between copayments and coinsurances for mental health care and all other illnesses. For example, outpatient mental health care had a 50 percent coinsurance payment while office visits for other illnesses had a $10 copayment.
[4] Includes treatment in one or more of the following: outpatient department of a hospital, residential treatment center, organized outpatient clinic, day-night treatment center, or doctor's office. If benefits differed by location of treatment, doctor's office care was tabulated.

NOTE: Sum of individual items is greater than total because some participants were in plans with more than one type of limit. Where applicable, dash indicates no employees in this category, or data do not meet publication criteria.

**Table 40. Mental health care benefits: Separate limits on coverage in non-health maintenance organizations, full-time employees, private industry, National Compensation Survey, 2000**

| Coverage limitation | All employees | Professional, technical, and related employees | Clerical and sales employees | Blue-collar and service employees |
|---|---|---|---|---|
| Number (in thousands) with inpatient mental health care benefits .................... | 30,568 | 7,676 | 8,335 | 14,557 |
| Number (in thousands) with outpatient mental health care benefits .................... | 29,506 | 7,192 | 8,100 | 14,214 |
| Percent | | | | |
| **Inpatient care** | | | | |
| Total with mental health care benefits ........................... | 100 | 100 | 100 | 100 |
| No separate limits[1] .......... | 15 | 14 | 15 | 15 |
| Subject to separate limits[2] | 85 | 86 | 85 | 85 |
| Days ........................... | 75 | 72 | 74 | 77 |
| Dollars ........................ | 11 | 11 | 11 | 11 |
| Coinsurance ................ | 15 | 13 | 15 | 15 |
| Copayment ............ | 2 | 2 | 4 | 2 |
| Other[3] ........................ | 5 | 6 | 7 | 3 |
| **Outpatient care[4]** | | | | |
| Total with mental health care benefits ........................... | 100 | 100 | 100 | 100 |
| No separate limits[1] .......... | 7 | 5 | 5 | 8 |
| Subject to separate limits[2] | 93 | 95 | 95 | 92 |
| Days ........................... | 70 | 75 | 72 | 66 |
| Dollars ........................ | 19 | 21 | 13 | 20 |
| Coinsurance ................ | 28 | 25 | 30 | 30 |
| Copayment .................. | 20 | 25 | 21 | 18 |
| Other[3] ........................ | 22 | 13 | 27 | 23 |

[1] These include plans that provide coverage without any separate limits; they also include plans that provide coverage subject to only the major medical limits of the plan.

[2] Separate limitations indicate that mental health care benefits are more restrictive than benefits for other treatments. For example, if a plan limits inpatient mental health care to 30 days per year, that plan contains separate limits. The total is less than the sum of the individual items because many plans had more than one type of limitation.

[3] These are plans when comparisons were made between copayments and coinsurances for mental health care and all other illnesses. For example, outpatient mental health care had a 50 percent coinsurance payment while office visits for other illnesses had a $10 copayment.

[4] Includes treatment in one or more of the following: outpatient department of a hospital, residential treatment center, organized outpatient clinic, day-night treatment center, or doctor's office. If benefits differed by location of treatment, doctor's office care was tabulated.

NOTE: Sum of individual items is greater than total because some participants were in plans with more than one type of limit. Where applicable, dash indicates no employees in this category, or data do not meet publication criteria.

**Table 41. Alcohol and drug abuse treatment benefits: Relationship between provisions, full-time employees, National Compensation Survey, private industry, 2000**

| Relationship of coverage | All employees | Professional, technical, and related employees | Clerical and sales employees | Blue-collar and service employees |
|---|---|---|---|---|
| Number (in thousands) with medical care ...................... | 52,627 | 13,833 | 14,890 | 23,905 |
| Percent | | | | |
| Total ................................ | 100 | 100 | 100 | 100 |
| Covered together[1] ............... | 78 | 74 | 76 | 81 |
| Covered separately but with the same limits[3] ............. | 1 | 3 | 1 | ([2]) |
| Other[4] ............................... | 14 | 16 | 15 | 12 |
| Not determinable ................. | 7 | 6 | 8 | 7 |

[1] These are plans where all limits that apply to alcohol abuse treatment also apply to drug abuse treatment. When care is received for one of these types of treatment, it reduces the availability of care from the other. For example, if alcohol and drug abuse treatments are limited to 30 days per year and 20 days are used for alcohol abuse treatment, then there are 10 days left for drug abuse treatment.

[2] Less than 0.5 percent.

[3] These are plans where alcohol and drug abuse treatments are subject to separate but identical limits. For example, alcohol abuse treatment is limited to 30 days per year and drug abuse treatment is limited to a separate 30 days per year.

[4] Includes plans where alcohol abuse treatment coverage differs from drug abuse treatment coverage.

NOTE: Because of rounding, sums of individual items may not equal totals. Where applicable, dash indicates no employees in this category, or data do not meet publication criteria.

**Table 42. Substance abuse treatment benefits: Relationship to coverage for other illnesses, full-time employees, private industry, National Compensation Survey, 2000**

| Relationship to coverage for other illnesses | All employees | Professional, technical, and related employees | Clerical and sales employees | Blue-collar and service employees |
|---|---|---|---|---|
| | Percent | | | |
| **Alcohol abuse** | | | | |
| Total with inpatient detoxification[1] ................ | 100 | 100 | 100 | 100 |
| Covered the same .................... | 26 | 27 | 26 | 25 |
| Covered differently .................. | 74 | 73 | 74 | 75 |
| | | | | |
| Total with inpatient rehabilitation[2] ................ | 100 | 100 | 100 | 100 |
| Covered the same .................... | 7 | 8 | 8 | 6 |
| Covered differently .................. | 93 | 92 | 92 | 94 |
| | | | | |
| Total with outpatient rehabilitation[3] ................ | 100 | 100 | 100 | 100 |
| Covered the same .................... | 8 | 12 | 6 | 8 |
| Covered differently .................. | 92 | 88 | 94 | 92 |
| **Drug abuse** | | | | |
| Total with inpatient detoxification[1] ................ | 100 | 100 | 100 | 100 |
| Covered the same .................... | 26 | 26 | 25 | 26 |
| Covered differently .................. | 74 | 74 | 75 | 74 |
| | | | | |
| Total with inpatient rehabilitation[2] ................ | 100 | 100 | 100 | 100 |
| Covered the same .................... | 7 | 7 | 8 | 6 |
| Covered differently .................. | 93 | 93 | 92 | 94 |
| | | | | |
| Total with outpatient rehabilitation[3] ................ | 100 | 100 | 100 | 100 |
| Covered the same .................... | 8 | 11 | 6 | 8 |
| Covered differently .................. | 92 | 89 | 94 | 92 |

[1] Detoxification is the systematic use of medication and other methods under medical supervision to reduce or eliminate the effects of substance abuse.
[2] Rehabilitation is designed to alter the abusive behavior in patients once they are free of acute physical and mental complications.
[3] Includes treatment in one or more of the following: outpatient department of a hospital, residential treatment center, organized outpatient clinic, day-night treatment center, or doctor's office. If benefits differed by location of treatment, the location offering the most beneficial coverage was tabulated.

NOTE: Because of rounding, sums of individual items may not equal totals. Where applicable, dash indicates no employees in this category, or data do not meet publication criteria.

**Table 43. Alcohol abuse treatment benefits: Separate limits on coverage, full-time employees, private industry, National Compensation Survey, 2000**

| Coverage limitation | All employees | Professional, technical, and related employees | Clerical and sales employees | Blue-collar and service employees |
|---|---|---|---|---|
| Number (in thousands) with inpatient detoxification benefits .............................. | 49,703 | 13,074 | 14,030 | 22,598 |
| Number (in thousands) with inpatient rehabilitation benefits .............................. | 41,868 | 10,908 | 11,918 | 19,043 |
| Number (in thousands) with outpatient rehabilitation benefits .............................. | 44,840 | 11,710 | 12,468 | 20,661 |
| | Percent | | | |
| **Inpatient detoxification[1]** | | | | |
| Total with inpatient detoxification benefits ..... | 100 | 100 | 100 | 100 |
| No separate limits[2] .......... | 27 | 29 | 27 | 27 |
| Subject to separate limits[3] | 73 | 71 | 73 | 73 |
| Days ............................ | 53 | 53 | 55 | 52 |
| Dollars .......................... | 27 | 22 | 23 | 33 |
| Coinsurance ................ | 7 | 8 | 8 | 7 |
| Copayment ................. | 3 | 4 | 3 | 3 |
| Other[4] .......................... | 5 | 5 | 7 | 4 |
| **Inpatient rehabilitation[5]** | | | | |
| Total with inpatient rehabilitation benefits ...... | 100 | 100 | 100 | 100 |
| No separate limits[2] .......... | 8 | 9 | 9 | 6 |
| Subject to separate limits[3] | 92 | 91 | 91 | 94 |
| Days ............................ | 67 | 68 | 67 | 67 |
| Dollars .......................... | 32 | 26 | 28 | 38 |
| Coinsurance ................ | 11 | 10 | 13 | 10 |
| Copayment ................. | 5 | 6 | 5 | 4 |
| Other[4] .......................... | 7 | 6 | 9 | 5 |
| **Outpatient rehabilitation** | | | | |
| Total with outpatient rehabilitation benefits ...... | 100 | 100 | 100 | 100 |
| No separate limits[2] .......... | 9 | 12 | 7 | 8 |
| Subject to separate limits[3] | 91 | 88 | 93 | 92 |
| Days ............................ | 61 | 63 | 64 | 59 |
| Dollars .......................... | 34 | 29 | 30 | 39 |
| Coinsurance ................ | 16 | 12 | 17 | 18 |
| Copayment ................. | 21 | 25 | 25 | 17 |
| Other[4] .......................... | 17 | 11 | 23 | 17 |

See footnotes at end of table.

[1] Detoxification is the systematic use of medication and other methods under medical supervision to reduce or eliminate the effects of substance abuse.

[2] These include plans that provide coverage without any separate limits; they also include plans that provide coverage subject to only the major medical limits of the plan.

[3] Separate limitations indicate that alcohol abuse treatment benefits are more restrictive than benefits for other treatments. For example, if a plan limits inpatient rehabilitation care to 30 days per year, but the limit on inpatient care for any other type of illness is greater than 30 days per year, the plan contains separate limits. The total is less than the sum of the individual items because many plans had more than one type of limitation.

[4] These are plans when comparisons were made between copayments and coinsurances for alcohol abuse treatment and all other illnesses. For example, outpatient alcohol abuse treatment had a 50 percent coinsurance payment while office visits for other illnesses had a $10 copayment.

[5] Rehabilitation is designed to alter the abusive behavior in patients once they are free of acute physical and mental complications.

NOTE: Sum of individual items is greater than total because some participants were in plans with more than one type of limit. Where applicable, dash indicates no employees in this category, or data do not meet publication criteria.

**Table 44. Drug abuse treatment benefits: Separate limits on coverage, full-time employees, private industry, National Compensation Survey, 2000**

| Coverage limitation | All employees | Professional, technical, and related employees | Clerical and sales employees | Blue-collar and service employees |
|---|---|---|---|---|
| Number (in thousands) with inpatient detoxification benefits ................. | 49,553 | 13,050 | 13,979 | 22,524 |
| Number (in thousands) with inpatient rehabilitation benefits ................. | 41,607 | 10,847 | 11,879 | 18,881 |
| Number (in thousands) with outpatient rehabilitation benefits ................. | 44,402 | 11,644 | 12,429 | 20,329 |
| Percent | | | | |
| **Inpatient detoxification[1]** | | | | |
| Total with inpatient detoxification benefits ..... | 100 | 100 | 100 | 100 |
| No separate limits[2] ........... | 27 | 28 | 27 | 27 |
| Subject to separate limits[3] | 73 | 72 | 73 | 73 |
| Days ............................ | 54 | 54 | 55 | 52 |
| Dollars ......................... | 27 | 22 | 24 | 33 |
| Coinsurance ................. | 7 | 7 | 8 | 7 |
| Copayment ................... | 3 | 4 | 3 | 3 |
| Other[4] ......................... | 5 | 5 | 7 | 4 |
| **Inpatient rehabilitation[5]** | | | | |
| Total with inpatient rehabilitation benefits ...... | 100 | 100 | 100 | 100 |
| No separate limits[2] ........... | 7 | 8 | 9 | 6 |
| Subject to separate limits[3] | 93 | 92 | 91 | 94 |
| Days ............................ | 68 | 69 | 68 | 67 |
| Dollars ......................... | 32 | 26 | 28 | 38 |
| Coinsurance ................. | 11 | 10 | 13 | 10 |
| Copayment ................... | 5 | 6 | 5 | 4 |
| Other[4] ......................... | 7 | 6 | 9 | 6 |

See footnotes at end of table.

**Table 44. Drug abuse treatment benefits: Separate limits on coverage, full-time employees, private industry, National Compensation Survey, 2000 — Continued**

| Coverage limitation | All employees | Professional, technical, and related employees | Clerical and sales employees | Blue-collar and service employees |
|---|---|---|---|---|
| **Outpatient rehabilitation[6]** | | | | |
| Total with outpatient rehabilitation benefits ...... | 100 | 100 | 100 | 100 |
| No separate limits[2] ........... | 8 | 11 | 6 | 8 |
| Subject to separate limits[3] | 92 | 89 | 94 | 92 |
| Days ............................ | 62 | 64 | 64 | 59 |
| Dollars ......................... | 34 | 29 | 30 | 39 |
| Coinsurance ................. | 16 | 12 | 17 | 17 |
| Copayment ................... | 21 | 25 | 24 | 17 |
| Other[4] ......................... | 17 | 11 | 23 | 17 |

[1] Detoxification is the systematic use of medication and other methods under medical supervision to reduce or eliminate the effects of substance abuse.

[2] These include plans that provide coverage without any separate limits; they also include plans that provide coverage subject to only the major medical limits of the plan.

[3] Separate limitations indicate that drug abuse treatment benefits are more restrictive than benefits for other treatments. For example, if a plan limits inpatient rehabilitation care to 30 days per year, but the limit on inpatient care for any other type of illness is greater than 30 days per year, the plan contains separate limits. The total is less than the sum of the individual items because many plans had more than one type of limitation.

[4] These are plans when comparisons were made between copayments and coinsurances for drug abuse treatment and all other illnesses. For example, outpatient drug abuse treatment had a 50 percent coinsurance payment while office visits for other illnesses had a $10 copayment.

[5] Rehabilitation is designed to alter the abusive behavior in patients once they are free of acute physical and mental complications.

[6] Includes treatment in one or more of the following: outpatient department of a hospital, residential treatment center, organized outpatient clinic, day-night treatment center, or doctor's office. If benefits differed by location of treatment, the location offering the most beneficial coverage was tabulated.

NOTE: Sum of individual items is greater than total because some participants were in plans with more than one type of limit. Where applicable, dash indicates no employees in this category, or data do not meet publication criteria.

| Coverage limitation | All employees | Professional, technical, and related employees | Clerical and sales employees | Blue-collar and service employees |
|---|---|---|---|---|
| Number (in thousands) with inpatient detoxification benefits | 30,006 | 7,551 | 8,328 | 14,128 |
| Number (in thousands) with inpatient rehabilitation benefits | 26,411 | 6,614 | 7,521 | 12,275 |
| Number (in thousands) with outpatient rehabilitation benefits | 27,133 | 6,612 | 7,462 | 13,059 |
| **Percent** | | | | |
| **Inpatient detoxification[1]** | | | | |
| Total with inpatient detoxification benefits | 100 | 100 | 100 | 100 |
| No separate limits[2] | 20 | 20 | 20 | 20 |
| Subject to separate limits[3] | 80 | 80 | 80 | 80 |
| Days | 60 | 61 | 61 | 59 |
| Dollars | 35 | 29 | 29 | 41 |
| Coinsurance | 9 | 10 | 10 | 9 |
| Copayment | 3 | 2 | 2 | 3 |
| Other[4] | 6 | 6 | 9 | 3 |
| **Inpatient rehabilitation[5]** | | | | |
| Total with inpatient rehabilitation benefits | 100 | 100 | 100 | 100 |
| No separate limits[2] | 6 | 4 | 8 | 6 |
| Subject to separate limits[3] | 94 | 96 | 92 | 94 |
| Days | 67 | 73 | 68 | 64 |
| Dollars | 38 | 33 | 32 | 45 |
| Coinsurance | 11 | 11 | 13 | 11 |
| Copayment | 2 | 2 | 3 | 3 |
| Other[4] | 7 | 8 | 11 | 4 |

See footnotes at end of table.

---

**Table 48. Drug abuse treatment benefits: Limits on cov... in non-health maintenance organizations, full-time empl... private industry, National Compensation Survey, 2000 — Continued**

| Coverage limitation | All employees | Professional, technical, and related employees | Clerical and sales employees | |
|---|---|---|---|---|
| **Outpatient rehabilitation[6]** | | | | |
| Total with outpatient rehabilitation benefits | 100 | 100 | 100 | |
| No separate limits[2] | 3 | 4 | 4 | |
| Subject to separate limits[3] | 97 | 96 | 96 | |
| Days | 62 | 68 | 64 | |
| Dollars | 41 | 38 | 36 | |
| Coinsurance | 23 | 19 | 24 | |
| Copayment | 15 | 21 | 17 | |
| Other[4] | 22 | 14 | 28 | |

[1] Detoxification is the systematic use of medication and other ... under medical supervision to reduce or eliminate the effects of su... abuse.
[2] These include plans that provide coverage without any separa... they also include plans that provide coverage subject to only th... medical limits of the plan.
[3] Separate limitations indicate that drug abuse treatment ben... more restrictive than benefits for other treatments. For example, i... limits inpatient rehabilitation care to 30 days per year, but the... inpatient care for any other type of illness is greater than 30 days ... the plan contains separate limits. The total is less than the sum... individual items because many plans had more than one type of limita...
[4] These are plans when comparisons were made between cop... and coinsurances for drug abuse treatment and all other illnesse... example, outpatient drug abuse treatment had a 50 percent coi... payment while office visits for other illnesses had a $10 copayment.
[5] Rehabilitation is designed to alter the abusive behavior in patie... they are free of acute physical and mental complications.
[6] Includes treatment in one or more of the following: o... department of a hospital, residential treatment center, organized o... clinic, day-night treatment center, or doctor's office. If benefits di... location of treatment, the location offering the most beneficial cover... tabulated.

NOTE: Sum of individual items is greater than total becaus... participants were in plans with more than one type of limit. Where ap... dash indicates no employees in this category, or data do not meet pu... criteria.

---

**Table 45. Alcohol abuse treatment benefits: Separate limits on coverage in health maintenance organizations, full-time employees, private industry, National Compensation Survey, 2000**

| Coverage limitation | All employees | Professional, technical, and related employees | Clerical and sales employees | Blue-collar and service employees |
|---|---|---|---|---|
| Number (in thousands) with inpatient detoxification benefits | 19,547 | 5,499 | 5,652 | 8,396 |
| Number (in thousands) with inpatient rehabilitation benefits | 15,196 | 4,233 | 4,357 | 6,606 |
| Number (in thousands) with outpatient rehabilitation benefits | 17,405 | 5,032 | 4,967 | 7,406 |
| **Percent** | | | | |
| **Inpatient detoxification[1]** | | | | |
| Total with inpatient detoxification benefits | 100 | 100 | 100 | 100 |
| No separate limits[2] | 40 | 42 | 38 | 40 |
| Subject to separate limits[3] | 60 | 58 | 62 | 60 |
| Days | 43 | 42 | 46 | 42 |
| Dollars | 15 | 11 | 15 | 19 |
| Coinsurance | 4 | 4 | 5 | 3 |
| Copayment | 5 | 8 | 4 | 3 |
| Other[4] | 5 | 4 | 4 | 6 |
| **Inpatient rehabilitation[5]** | | | | |
| Total with inpatient rehabilitation benefits | 100 | 100 | 100 | 100 |
| No separate limits[2] | 11 | 17 | 13 | 6 |
| Subject to separate limits[3] | 89 | 83 | 87 | 94 |
| Days | 68 | 61 | 67 | 73 |
| Dollars | 22 | 16 | 20 | 27 |
| Coinsurance | 10 | 8 | 14 | 8 |
| Copayment | 10 | 12 | 10 | 8 |
| Other[4] | 7 | 4 | 6 | 9 |

See footnotes at end of table.

---

**Table 45. Alcohol abuse treatment benefits: Separate limits on coverage in health maintenance organizations, full-time employees, private industry, National Compensation Survey, 2000 — Continued**

| Coverage limitation | All employees | Professional, technical, and related employees | Clerical and sales employees | Blue-collar and service employees |
|---|---|---|---|---|
| **Outpatient rehabilitation[6]** | | | | |
| Total with outpatient rehabilitation benefits | 100 | 100 | 100 | 100 |
| No separate limits[2] | 17 | 22 | 11 | 17 |
| Subject to separate limits[3] | 83 | 78 | 89 | 83 |
| Days | 61 | 57 | 64 | 62 |
| Dollars | 22 | 17 | 20 | 27 |
| Coinsurance | 6 | 4 | 7 | 7 |
| Copayment | 32 | 30 | 37 | 29 |
| Other[4] | 10 | 8 | 15 | 8 |

[1] Detoxification is the systematic use of medication and other methods under medical supervision to reduce or eliminate the effects of substance abuse.
[2] These include plans that provide coverage without any separate limits; they also include plans that provide coverage subject to only the major medical limits of the plan.
[3] Separate limitations indicate that alcohol abuse treatment benefits are more restrictive than benefits for other treatments. For example, if a plan limits inpatient rehabilitation care to 30 days per year, but the limit on inpatient care for any other type of illness is greater than 30 days per year, the plan contains separate limits. The total is less than the sum of the individual items because many plans had more than one type of limitation.
[4] These are plans when comparisons were made between copayments and coinsurances for alcohol abuse treatment and all other illnesses. For example, outpatient alcohol abuse treatment had a 50 percent coinsurance payment while office visits for other illnesses had a $10 copayment.
[5] Rehabilitation is designed to alter the abusive behavior in patients once they are free of acute physical and mental complications.
[6] Includes treatment in one or more of the following: outpatient department of a hospital, residential treatment center, organized outpatient clinic, day-night treatment center, or doctor's office. If benefits differed by location of treatment, the location offering the most beneficial coverage was tabulated.

NOTE: Sum of individual items is greater than total because some participants were in plans with more than one type of limit. Where applicable, dash indicates no employees in this category, or data do not meet publication criteria.

## Table 46. Drug abuse treatment benefits: Separate limits on coverage in health maintenance organizations, full-time employees, private industry, National Compensation Survey, 2000

| Coverage limitation | All employees | Professional, technical, and related employees | Clerical and sales employees | Blue-collar and service employees |
|---|---|---|---|---|
| Number (in thousands) with inpatient detoxification benefits | 19,547 | 5,499 | 5,652 | 8,396 |
| Number (in thousands) with inpatient rehabilitation benefits | 15,196 | 4,233 | 4,357 | 6,606 |
| Number (in thousands) with outpatient rehabilitation benefits | 17,269 | 5,032 | 4,967 | 7,270 |
| **Percent** | | | | |
| **Inpatient detoxification[1]** | | | | |
| Total with inpatient detoxification benefits | 100 | 100 | 100 | 100 |
| No separate limits[2] | 39 | 40 | 37 | 39 |
| Subject to separate limits[3] | 61 | 60 | 63 | 61 |
| Days | 44 | 44 | 47 | 42 |
| Dollars | 15 | 11 | 15 | 19 |
| Coinsurance | 4 | 4 | 5 | 3 |
| Copayment | 5 | 8 | 4 | 3 |
| Other[4] | 5 | 4 | 4 | 6 |
| **Inpatient rehabilitation[5]** | | | | |
| Total with inpatient rehabilitation benefits | 100 | 100 | 100 | 100 |
| No separate limits[2] | 10 | 15 | 11 | 6 |
| Subject to separate limits[3] | 90 | 85 | 89 | 94 |
| Days | 68 | 64 | 68 | 71 |
| Dollars | 22 | 16 | 20 | 27 |
| Coinsurance | 10 | 8 | 14 | 8 |
| Copayment | 10 | 12 | 10 | 8 |
| Other[4] | 7 | 4 | 6 | 9 |

See footnotes at end of table.

## Table 46. Drug abuse treatment benefits: Separate limits on coverage in health maintenance organizations, full-time employees, private industry, National Compensation Survey, 2000 — Continued

| Coverage limitation | All employees | Professional, technical, and related employees | Clerical and sales employees | Blue-collar and service employees |
|---|---|---|---|---|
| **Outpatient rehabilitation[6]** | | | | |
| Total with outpatient rehabilitation benefits | 100 | 100 | 100 | 100 |
| No separate limits[2] | 16 | 20 | 10 | 17 |
| Subject to separate limits[3] | 84 | 80 | 90 | 83 |
| Days | 62 | 59 | 66 | 62 |
| Dollars | 22 | 17 | 20 | 28 |
| Coinsurance | 5 | 4 | 7 | 5 |
| Copayment | 31 | 29 | 36 | 29 |
| Other[4] | 10 | 8 | 15 | 8 |

[1] Detoxification is the systematic use of medication and other methods under medical supervision to reduce or eliminate the effects of substance abuse.
[2] These include plans that provide coverage without any separate limits; they also include plans that provide coverage subject to only the major medical limits of the plan.
[3] Separate limitations indicate that drug abuse treatment benefits are more restrictive than benefits for other treatments. For example, if a plan limits inpatient rehabilitation care to 30 days per year, but the limit on inpatient care for any other type of illness is greater than 30 days per year, the plan contains separate limits. The total is less than the sum of the individual items because many plans had more than one type of limitation.
[4] These are plans when comparisons were made between copayments and coinsurances for drug abuse treatment and all other illnesses. For example, outpatient drug abuse treatment had a 50 percent coinsurance payment while office visits for other illnesses had a $10 copayment.
[5] Rehabilitation is designed to alter the abusive behavior in patients once they are free of acute physical and mental complications.
[6] Includes treatment in one or more of the following: outpatient department of a hospital, residential treatment center, organized outpatient clinic, day-night treatment center, or doctor's office. If benefits differed by location of treatment, the location offering the most beneficial coverage was tabulated.

NOTE: Sum of individual items is greater than total because some participants were in plans with more than one type of limit. Where applicable, dash indicates no employees in this category, or data do not meet publication criteria.

## Table 47. Alcohol abuse treatment benefits: Separate limits on coverage in non-health maintenance organizations, full-time employees, private industry, National Compensation Survey, 2000

| Coverage limitation | All employees | Professional, technical, and related employees | Clerical and sales employees | Blue-collar and service employees |
|---|---|---|---|---|
| Number (in thousands) with inpatient detoxification benefits | 30,155 | 7,575 | 8,378 | 14,202 |
| Number (in thousands) with inpatient rehabilitation benefits | 26,672 | 6,675 | 7,560 | 12,437 |
| Number (in thousands) with outpatient rehabilitation benefits | 27,435 | 6,679 | 7,501 | 13,255 |
| **Percent** | | | | |
| **Inpatient detoxification[1]** | | | | |
| Total with inpatient detoxification benefits | 100 | 100 | 100 | 100 |
| No separate limits[2] | 19 | 20 | 20 | 19 |
| Subject to separate limits[3] | 81 | 80 | 80 | 81 |
| Days | 60 | 61 | 60 | 59 |
| Dollars | 35 | 29 | 29 | 41 |
| Coinsurance | 10 | 10 | 10 | 9 |
| Copayment | 2 | 1 | 2 | 3 |
| Other[4] | 6 | 6 | 9 | 3 |
| **Inpatient rehabilitation[5]** | | | | |
| Total with inpatient rehabilitation benefits | 100 | 100 | 100 | 100 |
| No separate limits[2] | 6 | 4 | 7 | 6 |
| Subject to separate limits[3] | 94 | 96 | 93 | 94 |
| Days | 67 | 72 | 68 | 64 |
| Dollars | 38 | 33 | 32 | 44 |
| Coinsurance | 12 | 11 | 13 | 11 |
| Copayment | 2 | 2 | 2 | 3 |
| Other[4] | 7 | 8 | 11 | 4 |

See footnotes at end of table.

## Table 47. Alcohol abuse treatment benefits: Separate limits on coverage in non-health maintenance organizations, full-time employees, private industry, National Compensation Survey, 2000 — Continued

| Coverage limitation | All employees |
|---|---|
| **Outpatient rehabilitation[6]** | |
| Total with outpatient rehabilitation benefits | 100 |
| No separate limits[2] | 3 |
| Subject to separate limits[3] | 97 |
| Days | 61 |
| Dollars | 41 |
| Coinsurance | 23 |
| Copayment | 14 |
| Other[4] | 21 |

[1] Detoxification is the systematic use of medication and under medical supervision to reduce or eliminate the effec... abuse.
[2] These include plans that provide coverage without any s... they also include plans that provide coverage subject to on... medical limits of the plan.
[3] Separate limitations indicate that alcohol abuse treatment b... more restrictive than benefits for other treatments. For example,... limits inpatient rehabilitation care to 30 days per year, but the... inpatient care for any other type of illness is greater than 30 days p... the plan contains separate limits. The total is less than the sum... individual items because many plans had more than one type of limitati...
[4] These are plans when comparisons were made between copaym... and coinsurances for alcohol abuse treatment and all other illnesses.... example, outpatient alcohol abuse treatment had a 50 percent coinsura... payment while office visits for other illnesses had a $10 copayment.
[5] Rehabilitation is designed to alter the abusive behavior in patients onc... they are free of acute physical and mental complications.
[6] Includes treatment in one or more of the following: outpatient department of a hospital, residential treatment center, organized outpatient clinic, day-night treatment center, or doctor's office. If benefits differed by location of treatment, the location offering the most beneficial coverage was tabulated.

NOTE: Sum of individual items is greater than total because some participants were in plans with more than one type of limit. Where applicable, dash indicates no employees in this category, or data do not meet publication criteria.

**Table 49. Non-health mantenance organizations: Pre-existing condition provisions,[1] full-time employees, private industry, National Compensation Survey, 2000**

| Pre-existing condition provisions | All employees | Professional, technical, and related employees | Clerical and sales employees | Blue-collar and service employees |
|---|---|---|---|---|
| Number (in thousands) in non-HMO plans .................. | 32,733 | 8,269 | 9,180 | 15,283 |
| | Percent | | | |
| Total with non-HMO plans ........ | 100 | 100 | 100 | 100 |
| Pre-existing condition clause | 49 | 50 | 43 | 52 |
| No pre-existing condition clause ............................. | 43 | 39 | 48 | 42 |
| Not determinable .................. | 8 | 10 | 9 | 6 |

[1] A pre-existing condition is any ailment present at the time the participant enrolls in the plan. Plans will typically deny or limit coverage of such conditions for a specific time period following enrollment.

NOTE: Because of rounding, sums of individual items may not equal totals. Where applicable, dash indicates no employees in this category, or data do not meet publication criteria.

**Table 50. Dental care benefits: Fee arrangement and financial intermediary, full-time employees, private industry, National Compensation Survey, 2000**

| Fee arrangement | All employees | Professional, technical, and related employees | Clerical and sales employees | Blue-collar and service employees |
|---|---|---|---|---|
| Number (in thousands) with dental care .......................... | 30,352 | 9,202 | 8,783 | 12,367 |
| | Percent | | | |
| Total with dental care ............... | 100 | 100 | 100 | 100 |
| Traditional fee-for-service[1] ... | 60 | 59 | 57 | 63 |
| Self insured[2] ...................... | 38 | 31 | 34 | 46 |
| Fully insured ...................... | 19 | 27 | 18 | 15 |
| Combined financing .......... | 3 | 2 | 5 | 2 |
| Preferred provider organization[3] .................. | 25 | 26 | 26 | 23 |
| Self insured[2] ...................... | 13 | 12 | 13 | 14 |
| Fully insured ...................... | 12 | 14 | 13 | 9 |
| Health maintenance organization[4] .................. | 15 | 14 | 17 | 14 |
| Self insured[2] ...................... | 3 | 2 | 3 | 3 |
| Fully insured ...................... | 12 | 12 | 13 | 10 |
| Other[6] ................................... | ([5]) | ([5]) | ([5]) | - |

[1] These plans pay for specific dental procedures as expenses are incurred

[2] Includes plans that are financed on a pay-as-you-go basis, plans financed through contributions to a trust fund established to pay benefits, and plans operating their own facilities if at least partially financed by employer contributions. Includes plans that are administered by a commercial carrier through Administrative Services Only (ASO) contracts.

[3] A preferred provider organization (PPO) is a group of hospitals and dentists that contracts to provide comprehensive dental services. To encourage use of organization members, the dental care plan limits reimbursement rates when participants use nonmember services.

[4] Delivers comprehensive dental care on a prepayment rather than fee-for-service basis.

[5] Less than 0.5 percent.

[6] Includes exclusive provider organizations, which are groups of hospitals and dentists that contract to provide comprehensive dental services. Participants are required to obtain services from members of the organization in order to receive plan benefits.

NOTE: Because of rounding, sums of individual items may not equal totals. Where applicable, dash indicates no employees in this category, or data do not meet publication criteria.

**Table 51. Dental care benefits: Coverage for selected procedures, full-time employees, private industry, National Compensation Survey, 2000**

| Extent of coverage | Type of dental procedure | | | | | | | | |
|---|---|---|---|---|---|---|---|---|---|
| | Exams | X-rays | Surgery[1] | Fillings | Periodontal care | Endodontics | Crowns | Prosthetics | Orthodontia[2] |
| Number (in thousands) with dental care .............. | 30,352 | 30,352 | 30,352 | 30,352 | 30,352 | 30,352 | 30,352 | 30,352 | 30,352 |
| Professional, technical, and related employees .......... | 9,202 | 9,202 | 9,202 | 9,202 | 9,202 | 9,202 | 9,202 | 9,202 | 9,202 |
| Clerical and sales employees | 8,783 | 8,783 | 8,783 | 8,783 | 8,783 | 8,783 | 8,783 | 8,783 | 8,783 |
| Blue-collar and service employees ..................... | 12,367 | 12,367 | 12,367 | 12,367 | 12,367 | 12,367 | 12,367 | 12,367 | 12,367 |
| | Percent | | | | | | | | |
| **All employees** | | | | | | | | | |
| Total ............................... | 100 | 100 | 100 | 100 | 100 | 100 | 100 | 100 | 100 |
| Covered[3] ............................. | 100 | 100 | 100 | 100 | 100 | 100 | 99 | 99 | 68 |
| In full[4] ................................. | 15 | 15 | 3 | 7 | 5 | 4 | 1 | (5) | (5) |
| Scheduled cash allowance | 4 | 4 | 6 | 6 | 6 | 6 | 6 | 5 | 6 |
| Subject to copayment[6] ..... | 2 | 1 | 7 | 5 | 7 | 8 | 9 | 9 | 11 |
| Percent of usual, customary and reasonable charge ...... | 80 | 80 | 84 | 82 | 82 | 83 | 84 | 85 | 59 |
| Other[7] ............................... | (5) | (5) | (5) | 1 | (5) | (5) | 1 | 1 | 1 |
| Not covered .......................... | - | - | (5) | - | (5) | (5) | 1 | 1 | 28 |
| Not determinable .................. | - | - | (5) | - | - | - | - | - | 4 |
| **Professional, technical, and related employees** | | | | | | | | | |
| Total ............................... | 100 | 100 | 100 | 100 | 100 | 100 | 100 | 100 | 100 |
| Covered[3] ............................. | 100 | 100 | 100 | 100 | 99 | 100 | 98 | 98 | 67 |
| In full[4] ................................. | 13 | 14 | 1 | 4 | 1 | 1 | 1 | (5) | (5) |
| Scheduled cash allowance | 3 | 3 | 6 | 6 | 6 | 6 | 6 | 5 | 8 |
| Subject to copayment[6] ..... | 3 | 2 | 10 | 8 | 10 | 11 | 11 | 11 | 10 |
| Percent of usual, customary and reasonable charge ...... | 81 | 81 | 83 | 82 | 82 | 83 | 81 | 82 | 55 |
| Other[7] ............................... | (5) | (5) | (5) | (5) | (5) | (5) | (5) | (5) | 2 |
| Not covered .......................... | - | - | (5) | - | 1 | (5) | 2 | 2 | 27 |
| Not determinable .................. | - | - | (5) | - | - | - | - | - | 6 |

See footnotes at end of table.

**Table 51. Dental care benefits: Coverage for selected procedures, full-time employees, private industry, National Compensation Survey, 2000 — Continued**

| Extent of coverage | Type of dental procedure | | | | | | | | |
|---|---|---|---|---|---|---|---|---|---|
| | Exams | X-rays | Surgery[1] | Fillings | Periodontal care | Endodontics | Crowns | Prosthetics | Orthodontia[2] |
| | Percent | | | | | | | | |
| **Clerical and sales employees** | | | | | | | | | |
| Total ................................ | 100 | 100 | 100 | 100 | 100 | 100 | 100 | 100 | 100 |
| Covered[3] ........................... | 100 | 100 | 100 | 100 | 100 | 100 | 98 | 98 | 67 |
| In full[4] ........................... | 17 | 16 | 5 | 10 | 8 | 8 | 1 | 1 | ([5]) |
| Scheduled cash allowance | 2 | 2 | 5 | 4 | 5 | 5 | 5 | 4 | 6 |
| Subject to copayment[6] ..... | 2 | 2 | 4 | 4 | 4 | 5 | 7 | 6 | 9 |
| Percent of usual, customary and reasonable charge ...... | 80 | 80 | 87 | 83 | 84 | 84 | 87 | 88 | 60 |
| Other[7] ............................. | ([5]) | ([5]) | ([5]) | 1 | ([5]) | ([5]) | 1 | 1 | 2 |
| Not covered ......................... | - | - | ([5]) | - | ([5]) | ([5]) | 2 | 2 | 29 |
| Not determinable ................. | - | - | ([5]) | - | - | - | - | - | 4 |
| **Blue-collar and service employees** | | | | | | | | | |
| Total ................................ | 100 | 100 | 100 | 100 | 100 | 100 | 100 | 100 | 100 |
| Covered[3] ........................... | 100 | 100 | 99 | 100 | 99 | 100 | 100 | 100 | 70 |
| In full[4] ........................... | 15 | 15 | 4 | 7 | 5 | 2 | ([5]) | ([5]) | ([5]) |
| Scheduled cash allowance | 5 | 5 | 6 | 6 | 7 | 6 | 6 | 6 | 5 |
| Subject to copayment[6] ..... | 1 | 1 | 7 | 4 | 7 | 9 | 9 | 9 | 14 |
| Percent of usual, customary and reasonable charge ...... | 79 | 79 | 82 | 82 | 81 | 83 | 84 | 84 | 61 |
| Other[7] ............................. | ([5]) | ([5]) | 1 | 1 | 1 | 1 | 1 | 1 | 1 |
| Not covered ......................... | - | - | ([5]) | - | 1 | * | ([5]) | ([5]) | 28 |
| Not determinable ................. | - | - | ([5]) | - | - | - | - | - | £ |

[1] Excludes plans that limited coverage to accidental injuries, removal of impacted wisdom teeth, or repair of jaw.

[2] Participants were included as having coverage for orthodontia in cases where benefits were limited to children.

[3] Sum of individual items is greater than total because some participants were in plans with more than one limit.

[4] Includes plans that paid the full cost with no deductible or maximum dollar amount.

[5] Less than 0.5 percent.

[6] Participant pays a specific amount per procedure and plan pays all remaining expenses. In the case of orthodontia, the copayment is generally applied once per lifetime.

[7] Includes plans that provide care based on an incentive schedule or discounted benefit. An incentive schedule is a reimbursement arrangement in which the percentage of dental expenses paid by the plan increases if regular dental appointments are scheduled. Discounted benefits are available if obtained from an approved provider.

NOTE: Because of rounding, sums of individual items may not equal totals. Where applicable, dash indicates no employees in this category, or data do not meet publication criteria.

**Table 52. Dental care benefits: Percent of charges paid by plan for selected procedures, full-time employees, private industry, National Compensation Survey, 2000**

| Percent of usual, customary, and reasonable charge | Type of dental procedure | | | | | | | | |
|---|---|---|---|---|---|---|---|---|---|
| | Exams | X-rays | Surgery[1] | Fillings | Periodontal care | Endodontics | Crowns | Prosthetics | Orthodontia |
| Number of employees (in thousands) in dental plans with coverage based on a percentage of charges ............ | 24,158 | 24,323 | 25,442 | 24,960 | 24,935 | 25,211 | 25,507 | 25,662 | 17,811 |
| Professional, technical, and related employees | 7,433 | 7,447 | 7,636 | 7,545 | 7,580 | 7,612 | 7,464 | 7,569 | 5,020 |
| Clerical and sales employees ................. | 6,983 | 7,059 | 7,645 | 7,248 | 7,343 | 7,393 | 7,673 | 7,707 | 5,237 |
| Blue-collar and service employees ................. | 9,743 | 9,816 | 10,161 | 10,167 | 10,012 | 10,206 | 10,370 | 10,387 | 7,554 |
| | Percent | | | | | | | | |
| **All employees** | | | | | | | | | |
| Total with dental care based on a percentage of charges[2] ......................... | 100 | 100 | 100 | 100 | 100 | 100 | 100 | 100 | 100 |
| 50 ...................................... | (3) | (3) | 4 | 3 | 7 | 5 | 67 | 71 | 87 |
| 60 ...................................... | - | - | (3) | (3) | 1 | (3) | 13 | 13 | 6 |
| 80 ...................................... | 12 | 13 | 70 | 69 | 66 | 67 | 9 | 8 | 3 |
| 100[4] ................................ | 82 | 80 | 8 | 10 | 8 | 9 | 4 | 3 | 2 |
| **Professional, technical, and related employees** | | | | | | | | | |
| Total with dental care based on a percentage of charges[2] ......................... | 100 | 100 | 100 | 100 | 100 | 100 | 100 | 100 | 100 |
| 50 ...................................... | (3) | (3) | 4 | 3 | 7 | 6 | 68 | 70 | 87 |
| 60 ...................................... | - | - | (3) | (3) | 1 | (3) | 15 | 16 | 5 |
| 80 ...................................... | 8 | 9 | 67 | 68 | 64 | 65 | 5 | 4 | 3 |
| 100[4] ................................ | 89 | 87 | 13 | 14 | 13 | 14 | 8 | 8 | 3 |
| **Clerical and sales employees** | | | | | | | | | |
| Total with dental care based on a percentage of charges[2] ......................... | 100 | 100 | 100 | 100 | 100 | 100 | 100 | 100 | 100 |
| 50 ...................................... | (3) | (3) | 6 | 3 | 9 | 7 | 71 | 74 | 88 |
| 60 ...................................... | - | - | 1 | 1 | 1 | 1 | 11 | 11 | 8 |
| 80 ...................................... | 13 | 14 | 74 | 73 | 71 | 71 | 11 | 8 | 1 |
| 100[4] ................................ | 80 | 79 | 4 | 5 | 5 | 6 | 3 | 2 | 2 |

See footnotes at end of table.

**Table 52. Dental care benefits: Percent of charges paid by plan for selected procedures, full-time employees, private industry, National Compensation Survey, 2000 — Continued**

| Percent of usual, customary, and reasonable charge | Type of dental procedure | | | | | | | | |
|---|---|---|---|---|---|---|---|---|---|
| | Exams | X-rays | Surgery[1] | Fillings | Periodon- tal care | Endodon- tics | Crowns | Prosthet- ics | Ortho- dontia |
| | Percent | | | | | | | | |
| **Blue-collar and service employees** | | | | | | | | | |
| Total with dental care based on a percentage of charges[2] | 100 | 100 | 100 | 100 | 100 | 100 | 100 | 100 | 100 |
| 50 | ([3]) | ([3]) | 2 | 2 | 5 | 3 | 65 | 69 | 86 |
| 60 | - | - | ([3]) | ([3]) | 1 | ([3]) | 13 | 13 | 4 |
| 80 | 14 | 14 | 69 | 66 | 65 | 66 | 10 | 11 | 5 |
| 100[4] | 79 | 76 | 7 | 10 | 7 | 9 | 3 | 1 | 2 |

[1] Excludes plans that limited coverage to accidental injuries, removal of impacted wisdom teeth, or repair of jaw.
[2] Includes other percentages not presented separately.
[3] Less than 0.5 percent.
[4] Includes plans that paid 100 percent of charges, but imposed a deductible and limited payment to a maximum dollar amount.

NOTE: Because of rounding, sums of individual items may not equal totals. Where applicable, dash indicates no employees in this category, or data do not meet publication criteria.

**Table 53. Dental care benefits: Amount of individual deductibles,[1] full-time employees, private industry, National Compensation Survey, 2000**

| Type of deductible | All employees | Professional, technical, and related employees | Clerical and sales employees | Blue-collar and service employees |
|---|---|---|---|---|
| Number (in thousands) with dental care ........................... | 30,352 | 9,202 | 8,783 | 12,367 |
| | Percent | | | |
| Total with dental care .......... | 100 | 100 | 100 | 100 |
| Subject to separate dental deductible[2] ....................... | 70 | 75 | 68 | 68 |
| Yearly deductible only .... | 68 | 73 | 67 | 65 |
| $25 .......................... | 20 | 22 | 17 | 20 |
| $50 .......................... | 39 | 43 | 40 | 35 |
| Other ....................... | 9 | 8 | 10 | 10 |
| Lifetime deductible only .. | 1 | 1 | ([3]) | 2 |
| Both yearly and lifetime deductibles .............. | 1 | 1 | ([3]) | 1 |
| No deductible .......................... | 30 | 25 | 32 | 32 |
| Not determinable .................... | ([3]) | ([3]) | ([3]) | – |
| | Average[4] | | | |
| Average employee yearly deductible ............................ | $48 | $46 | $50 | $47 |

**Table 54. Dental care benefits: Relationship of yearly family deductibles to yearly individual deductibles, full-time employees, private industry, National Compensation Survey, 2000**

| Relationship | All employees | Professional, technical, and related employees | Clerical and sales employees | Blue-collar and service employees |
|---|---|---|---|---|
| Number (in thousands) with dental care .......................... | 30,352 | 9,202 | 8,783 | 12,367 |
| | Percent | | | |
| Total with dental care ......... | 100 | 100 | 100 | 100 |
| With individual and family deductible ........................... | 48 | 53 | 48 | 44 |
| Family deductible is: 2 times individual deductible .................. | 11 | 11 | 10 | 10 |
| 3 times individual deductible .................. | 35 | 41 | 35 | 32 |
| Other ................................. | 2 | 1 | 3 | 2 |
| No individual or family deductible ........................... | 52 | 47 | 52 | 56 |

NOTE: Because of rounding, sums of individual items may not equal totals. Where applicable, dash indicates no employees in this category, or data do not meet publication criteria.

[1] Amount of deductible described is for each insured person. In some plans, the individual and family deductibles are identical. Excludes separate deductibles for orthodontic procedures.
[2] A single deductible may not apply to all covered dental procedures. If separate deductibles applied to different procedures, the sum of the deductible amounts was tabulated.
[3] Less than 0.5 percent.
[4] The average is presented for all covered workers; averages exclude workers without the plan provision.

NOTE: Because of rounding, sums of individual items may not equal totals. Where applicable, dash indicates no employees in this category, or data do not meet publication criteria.

**Table 55. Dental care benefits: Services covered by deductible[1] provision, full-time employees, private industry, National Compensation Survey, 2000**

| Categories of care | All employees | Professional, technical, and related employees | Clerical and sales employees | Blue-collar and service employees |
|---|---|---|---|---|
| Number (in thousands) with dental deductible ................. | 20,838 | 6,796 | 5,941 | 8,102 |
| | Percent | | | |
| Total with a dental deductible | 100 | 100 | 100 | 100 |
| All categories[2] ........................ | 15 | 13 | 12 | 20 |
| All except exams and x-rays ... | 53 | 58 | 56 | 46 |
| All except exams, x-rays, and orthodontia ........................ | 22 | 22 | 19 | 25 |
| All except orthodontia ............. | 7 | 2 | 11 | 7 |
| Other[3] ..................................... | 3 | 5 | 2 | 3 |

[1] Includes plans with both a yearly deductible only, and a yearly and lifetime deductible.

[2] This applies to all categories of care covered by the plan. The categories of dental care are exams, x-rays, surgery, fillings, periodontal care, endodontics, crowns, prosthetics, and orthodontia.

[3] Includes other category combinations.

NOTE: Because of rounding, sums of individual items may not equal totals. Where applicable, dash indicates no employees in this category, or data do not meet publication criteria

**Table 56. Dental care benefits: Maximum benefit provisions,[1] full-time employees, private industry, National Compensation Survey, 2000**

| Dollar amount[2] | All employees | Professional, technical, and related employees | Clerical and sales employees | Blue-collar and service employees |
|---|---|---|---|---|
| Number (in thousands) with dental care .......................... | 30,352 | 9,202 | 8,783 | 12,367 |
| | Percent | | | |
| Total with dental care ......... | 100 | 100 | 100 | 100 |
| Yearly maximum specified[3] ...... | 81 | 84 | 80 | 78 |
| Less than $1,000 ................... | 4 | 6 | 4 | 3 |
| $1,000 ................................. | 35 | 34 | 35 | 37 |
| $1,001-$1,499 ....................... | 4 | 4 | 4 | 5 |
| $1,500 ................................. | 28 | 30 | 30 | 27 |
| Greater than $1,500 ............. | 8 | 11 | 8 | 6 |
| No yearly maximum .................. | 19 | 16 | 19 | 22 |
| Maximum provision not determinable ....................... | ([4]) | ([4]) | 1 | ([4]) |
| | Average[5] | | | |
| Average yearly maximum ......... | $1,275 | $1,297 | $1,280 | $1,253 |

[1] Includes all covered dental procedures except orthodontia  Amount of maximum specified is for each insured person.

[2] Coverage for dental procedures may also be subject to scheduled allowance, deductible, or coinsurance provisions in addition to maximum dollar limitations.

[3] If separate yearly maximums applied to different procedures, the sum of the maximums was tabulated. Maximums applied to dental expenses only.

[4] Less than 0.5 percent.

[5] The average is presented for all covered workers; averages exclude workers without the plan provision.

NOTE: Because of rounding, sums of individual items may not equal totals. Where applicable, dash indicates no employees in this category, or data do not meet publication criteria.

**Table 57. Orthodontic care benefits: Maximum benefit provisions, full-time employees, private industry, National Compensation Survey, 2000**

| Dollar amount[1] | All em-ploy-ees | Profes-sional, techni-cal, and related em-ploy-ees | Clerical and sales em-ploy-ees | Blue-collar and service em-ploy-ees |
|---|---|---|---|---|
| Number (in thousands) with orthodontic care .................. | 21,885 | 6,682 | 6,265 | 8,938 |
| Percent | | | | |
| Total with orthodontic care | 100 | 100 | 100 | 100 |
| Lifetime maximum specified .... | 76 | 78 | 74 | 76 |
| Less than $1,000 .................. | 7 | 5 | 9 | 8 |
| $1,000 ................................. | 33 | 26 | 35 | 38 |
| $1,001-$1,499 ...................... | 5 | 5 | 3 | 6 |
| $1,500 ................................. | 22 | 30 | 19 | 17 |
| Greater than $1,500 ............. | 8 | 11 | 7 | 7 |
| Dollar amount unspecified .... | ([2]) | 1 | ([2]) | ([2]) |
| No lifetime maximum ............... | 18 | 14 | 20 | 21 |
| Provision not determinable ....... | 5 | 8 | 6 | 3 |
| Average[3] | | | | |
| Average lifetime maximum ....... | $1,227 | $1,335 | $1,187 | $1,177 |

[1] Coverage for orthodontia procedure may also be subject to scheduled allowance, deductible, or coinsurance provisions in addition to maximum dollar limitations.

[2] Less than 0.5 percent.

[3] The average is presented for all covered workers; averages exclude workers without the plan provision.

NOTE: Because of rounding, sums of individual items may not equal totals. Where applicable, dash indicates no employees in this category, or data do not meet publication criteria.

**Table 58. Dental care benefits: Pretreatment authorization provisions, full-time employees, private industry, National Compensation Survey, 2000**

| Preauthorization provision | All em-ploy-ees | Profes-sional, techni-cal, and related em-ploy-ees | Clerical and sales em-ploy-ees | Blue-collar and service emplo-yees |
|---|---|---|---|---|
| Number (in thousands) with dental care ......................... | 30,352 | 9,202 | 8,783 | 12,367 |
| Percent | | | | |
| Total with dental care ......... | 100 | 100 | 100 | 100 |
| Preauthorization required ......... Minimum expense requiring preauthorization: | 49 | 46 | 46 | 52 |
| Less than $200 ................. | 5 | 4 | 4 | 7 |
| $200-$299 ...................... | 17 | 20 | 17 | 14 |
| $300 or more ................... | 21 | 16 | 22 | 24 |
| Dollar amount unspecified | 6 | 7 | 3 | 8 |
| Preauthorization not required ... | 40 | 37 | 44 | 39 |
| Provision not determinable ....... | 12 | 17 | 10 | 9 |
| Average[1] | | | | |
| Average minimum expense requiring preauthorization ... | $261 | $260 | $265 | $260 |

[1] The average is presented for all covered workers; averages exclude workers without the plan provision.

NOTE: Because of rounding, sums of individual items may not equal totals. Where applicable, dash indicates no employees in this category, or data do not meet publication criteria.

**Table 59. Vision care benefits: Coverage for selected services, full-time employees, private industry, National Compensation Survey, 2000**

| Type of vision benefit | Total | Covered[1] | Covered in full | Scheduled allowance | Copayment | Other[2] | Not covered | Not determinable |
|---|---|---|---|---|---|---|---|---|
| | | | | Percent | | | | |
| **All employees** | | | | | | | | |
| Eye exam ........................... | 100 | 99 | 20 | 29 | 45 | 14 | 1 | - |
| Contact lenses[3] ................... | 100 | 95 | 3 | 67 | 19 | 28 | 4 | 1 |
| Eyeglasses ......................... | 100 | 100 | 12 | 55 | 24 | 28 | - | - |
| **Professional, technical, and related employees** | | | | | | | | |
| Eye exam ........................... | 100 | 99 | 24 | 35 | 37 | 19 | 1 | - |
| Contact lenses[3] ................... | 100 | 95 | 2 | 75 | 13 | 35 | 2 | 3 |
| Eyeglasses ......................... | 100 | 100 | 15 | 59 | 21 | 34 | - | - |
| **Clerical and sales employees** | | | | | | | | |
| Eye exam ........................... | 100 | 100 | 22 | 24 | 48 | 14 | ([4]) | - |
| Contact lenses[3] ................... | 100 | 95 | 5 | 61 | 25 | 27 | 4 | ([4]) |
| Eyeglasses ......................... | 100 | 100 | 12 | 52 | 27 | 24 | - | - |
| **Blue-collar and service employees** | | | | | | | | |
| Eye exam ........................... | 100 | 99 | 16 | 28 | 49 | 11 | 1 | - |
| Contact lenses[3] ................... | 100 | 95 | 3 | 65 | 19 | 24 | 5 | - |
| Eyeglasses ......................... | 100 | 100 | 9 | 53 | 25 | 26 | - | - |

[1] The total is less than the sum of individual items because many participants are in plans with more than one type of limitation.

[2] Includes plans subject to coinsurance and retail discount.

[3] Includes plans that provide coverage for elected contact lenses, medically necessary contact lenses, i.e., cataract surgery, is normally provided under the surgical portion of the medical plan and is not described in this table.

[4] Less than 0.5 percent.

NOTE: Because of rounding, sums of individual items may not equal totals. Where applicable, dash indicates no employees in this category.

# Chapter 3.  Retirement Income Benefits

Defined benefit pension plans provide employees with guaranteed retirement benefits based on predetermined benefit formulas.  A participant's retirement age, length of service, and preretirement earnings may affect the benefits received.  Definitions, key provisions, and related terms follow.

## Benefit formulas

*Terminal earnings formulas.*  Benefits are based on a percentage of average earnings during a specified number of years at the end of a worker's career (or when earnings are highest) multiplied by the number of years of service recognized by the plan.

*Career-earnings formulas.*  Benefits are based on a percentage of an average of career earnings for every year of service recognized by the plan.

*Dollar amount formulas.*  Benefits are based on a dollar amount for each year of service recognized by the plan.

*Cash account formulas.*  Benefits are computed as a percent of each employee's account balance.  Employers specify a contribution, and a rate of interest on that contribution, that will provide a predetermined amount at retirement.

*Percent of contribution formulas.*  Benefits are based on employer, and, occasionally, employee contributions.  Benefits equal a percent of total contributions.

## Normal retirement

Normal retirement is the age at which plan participants could retire and receive all accrued benefits.

## Early retirement

Early retirement is the age (or a combination of age and service) at which plan participants could retire and receive all accrued benefits less a reduction for the years prior to their normal retirement age.

## Benefit payment methods

Payments from defined benefit plans may be in the form of a straight-life annuity, joint-and-survivor annuity, percent of unreduced accrued benefit, or a lump sum.

*Straight life annuity.*  A periodic payment made for the life of the retiree, with no additional payments to survivors.

*Joint and survivor annuity.*  The Employee Retirement Income Security Act of 1974 (ERISA) requires defined benefit pension plans that offer an annuity as a payment option to provide a qualified joint and survivor annuity (QJSA) as the normal benefit payment for married participants.  A QJSA is an immediate annuity for the life of the participant and a survivor annuity for the life of the participant's spouse.  The amount of the survivor annuity may not be less than 50 percent nor more than 100 percent of the amount payable during the time that the participant and spouse are both alive.  The annuity payable for the life of the participant is lower than that for a straight-life annuity.  To account for the increased length of time over which payments will be made, this reduction may be a percent of the straight-life benefit, such as 10 percent, or based on the life expectancy of the participant and spouse (the so-called actuarial reduction).

*Percent of unreduced accrued benefit.*  Under this method, the participant's pension is not reduced to adjust for survivor benefits.  The participant will receive an amount equal to the straight-life annuity and the spouse will receive a proportion of that amount, often 50 percent, should the participant die.

*Lump-sum payment.*  The participant may opt for a full-lump sum, with no further benefits received from the plan.  If a plan provides for a partial lump-sum payment, the participant will usually receive a reduced annuity as well.

## Vesting

Vesting refers to the amount of time a participant must work before earning a nonforfeitable right to a retirement benefit.  Once vested, the accrued benefit is retained even if the worker leaves the employer before reaching retirement age.

*Cliff vesting.*  No vesting occurs until an employee satisfies the service requirements for 100-percent vesting, for example after 5 years.

*Graduated vesting.*  An employee's nonforfeitable percentage of employer contributions increases over time until vesting reaches 100 percent.

## Integration with Social Security

Defined benefit plans may "integrate" retirement benefits with Social Security benefits. Under this approach the employer's contribution to Social Security (FICA taxes) is taken into account when computing plan benefits. Integration may be accomplished by an offset or a step-rate method.

*Offset.* Part of a participant's Social Security benefit is subtracted from the benefit otherwise payable by the plan. The maximum allowable offset is half of the annual Social Security benefit.

*Step-rate.* Lower benefit rates are applied to earnings up to the specified taxable Social Security wage base (i.e., the earnings subject to Social Security tax) in a given year.

## Portability

Portability is a participant's ability to maintain and transfer accumulated pension benefits when changing jobs. Portability provisions in defined benefit plans generally cover portability of assets, portability of credited service, or both.

*Portability of assets.* Participants can withdraw their accumulated pension benefits and/or transfer them to another retirement arrangement.

*Portability of credited service.* Participants are allowed to count the years of service with a previous employer when determining benefits from a later employer.

## Disability retirement

Retirement resulting from a totally disabling injury or illness before a participant's eligibility for early or normal retirement. Plans providing disability retirement benefits may have a service requirement of 10 years or more. Benefits may be immediate or deferred.

## Post-retirement pension increases

Benefits received by retired participants may be adjusted to account for loss of purchasing power due to inflation. Some plans specify automatic cost-of-living increases, usually based on changes in the Consumer Price Index. Some employers provide discretionary or ad hoc increases to adjust retiree benefits for inflation.

## Defined Contribution Plans

Defined contribution plans are retirement plans that specify the level of employer contributions and place those contributions into individual employee accounts.

## Plan types

*Savings and thrift plans.* A retirement plan under which employees may contribute a predetermined portion of earnings (usually pretax) to an individual account, all or part of which the employer matches. Employers may match a fixed percent of employee contributions or a percent that varies by length of service, the amount of employee contribution, or other factors. Contributions are invested as directed by the employee or employer. Although usually designed as a long-term savings vehicle, savings and thrift plans may allow pre-retirement withdrawals and loans.

*Deferred profit-sharing plans.* A retirement plan under which a company credits a portion of company profits to employees' accounts. Plans may set a fixed formula for sharing profits, but this is not a requirement. Most plans hold money in employee accounts until retirement, disability, or death.

*Money purchase pension plans.* A retirement plan under which fixed employer contributions, typically calculated as a percentage of employee earnings, are allocated to individual employee accounts. Some plans may allow employee contributions, but employees are usually not required to make any contributions. Employers may also make profit-sharing contributions to these plans at their discretion.

*Employee Stock Ownership Plan (ESOP).* A retirement plan under which the employer pays a designated amount, often borrowed, into a fund which then invests primarily in company stock. Any debt incurred in the purchase of the stock is repaid by the company. Stock is then distributed to employees according to an allocation formula.

## Investment choices

*Company stock.* Employees receive equity in the company that sponsors the defined contribution plan.

*Common stock fund.* A professionally managed fund that invests in the common stock of a variety of companies.

*Fixed interest securities.* Bonds and other non-Federal instruments that pay a fixed interest rate over a period of time.

*Diversified investments.* Any professionally managed fund that invests in more than one type of equity or debt instrument.

*U.S. Government securities.* Treasury Bills, Treasury Notes, and Savings Bonds that pay a fixed rate of interest guaranteed by the U.S. government.

*Guaranteed Investment Contract (GIC).* An investment vehicle offered by insurance companies that guarantee the principal and a fixed rate of return for a specified time period.

*Money market fund.* A professionally managed mutual fund that buys high-quality, short-term notes, or certificates of deposit. The fund sells shares to investors who receive regular payments of interest.

*Certificate of deposit.* A receipt issued by banks or savings and loans associations for a deposit of funds. Interest accrues on the amount deposited and is paid at maturity.

## Withdrawals, loans, and distributions

*Withdrawals.* Prior to normal payout (usually at retirement), defined contribution plan participants may be allowed to withdraw all or a portion of the money in their accounts. While most early withdrawals incur tax penalties, hardship withdrawals do not. (See below.) To avoid tax penalties, many plans have loan provisions that allow employees to borrow from their accounts, with interest, for a specified period of time.

*Hardship withdrawals.* Employees are usually not penalized when money is withdrawn as a result of a hardship often defined as a death or illness of a family member, education expenses, sudden uninsured losses, or a need to prevent eviction from one's primary residence.

*Loans.* Defined contribution plans may allow participants to borrow money, with interest, from their accounts. Loan amounts are often limited to a portion of the account balance. They usually have to be repaid within 5 years, but longer payment periods may apply for home purchase or renovation loans.

*Transfers/rollovers.* A rollover is a direct payment of plan benefits from a defined contribution plan into an IRA or another employer's plan. In a direct rollover, the employee is not taxed on the payment until it is later withdrawn or distributed.

*Distribution.* At retirement, defined contribution plans normally allow for payout in the form of a lump sum, a lifetime annuity, or installments over a specified period. While there is no tax penalty if the distribution takes place after age $59^{1/2}$, the distribution is subject to ordinary income tax.

*Lump-sum distribution.* An immediate disbursement of employer and employee contributions and any investment earnings.

*Annuity.* Annuities are a form of distribution that provides periodic payments for various periods of time. Straight-life annuities provide payments, usually monthly, for the lifetime of a retiree. Joint-and-survivor annuities provide payments to a retiree, and upon the retiree's death, payments to a surviving spouse.

*Installment payments.* Employees receive payments from the employer at fixed intervals, for example equal payments over 5 years.

## Vesting

Vesting is the amount of time an individual must work before earning a nonforfeitable right to a retirement benefit. Once vested, the accrued benefit is retained even if the worker leaves the employer before reaching retirement age. While defined contribution plans are subject to the same vesting rules under the Employee Retirement Income Security Act as defined benefit plans, vesting schedules vary. Vesting schedules only apply to employer contributions; employee contributions (including pretax contributions) are always 100-percent vested.

*Immediate full vesting.* Employees are immediately eligible to receive 100 percent of employer contributions.

*Graduated vesting.* An employee's nonforfeitable percentage of employer contributions increases over time until vesting reaches 100 percent.

*Cliff vesting.* No vesting occurs until an employee satisfies the service requirements for 100-percent vesting, for example after 5 years.

*Class-year vesting.* Employees become fully vested in employer contributions made during a specific period after a period of time, often 3 years.

## Employer contribution methods

*Specified matching percent.* Common in savings and thrift plans, the employer matches a specified percent of employee contributions. The matching percent can vary by length of service, amount of employee contribution, and other factors.

*Fixed percent of profits formula.* Common in deferred profit-sharing plans, the employer contributes a fixed percent of total annual profits to the plan. For example, no matter what the level of profits, 5% are contributed to the plan. Profits may include those for the entire company or just those in a specific business unit. A variation of this formula is when employers set aside a "reserve amount" of profits, for example $1,000,000, and only pay a fixed percent on those profits above this amount into the employees' defined contribution plan.

*Percentage of employee earnings.* Common in money purchase plans, the employer contributes a fixed percent of each employee's earnings into their individual account.

## Related plans and terms

*Stock bonus plans.* Contributions are placed in a trust fund that invests in securities, including those of the employing company. These plans are either financed by the employer, or jointly by the employer and employee. Upon retirement or separation from the company, proceeds from the trust fund are paid out to eligible employees in the form of company stock or cash.

*TIAA-CREF Affiliation.* TIAA-CREF plans are provided to employees at educational institutions and non-profit educational associations. They are most commonly money purchase plans but may contain matching formulas.

*Internal Revenue Code (IRC) Section 401(k) plans.* Plan that allows employees to make pre-tax contributions into deferred compensation plans via salary reduction agreements. These arrangements are often associated with savings and thrift and other defined contribution plans.

*Discretionary profit sharing contributions.* Money purchase pension and savings and thrift plans may have features whereby the plan sponsor makes payments to the plan, in addition to their usual contributions, directly from company profits.

**Table 60. Defined benefit plans: Summary of plan provisions, full-time employees, private industry, National Compensation Survey, 2000**

| Provisions | All employees | Professional, technical, and related employees | Clerical and sales employees | Blue-collar and service employees |
|---|---|---|---|---|
| Number (in thousands) with defined benefit plan ............ | 19,225 | 5,794 | 5,179 | 8,252 |
| | Percent | | | |
| Total with defined benefit plan .. | 100 | 100 | 100 | 100 |
| **Basic provisions** | | | | |
| Employee contribution required ........................ | 5 | - | - | - |
| Benefits based on earnings .. | 61 | 59 | 67 | 60 |
| Benefits integrated with Social Security ................ | 41 | 35 | 49 | 40 |
| Benefits subject to maximum[1] ...................... | 35 | - | - | - |
| Early retirement benefits available ......................... | 77 | 69 | 78 | 81 |
| Disability retirement benefits available ........................ | 69 | - | - | - |
| Availability of lump sum benefits at retirement ...... | 43 | 44 , | 51 | 37 |
| Automatic cost-of-living increase ......................... | 7 | 4 | 6 | 9 |
| **Other provisions** | | | | |
| Early retirement supplement available ........................ | 12 | - | - | - |
| Minimum benefits provision .. | 3 | 3 | 3 | 4 |
| Early retirement requires employer approval .......... | 2 | 1 | ([2]) | 3 |
| Deferred vested benefits available prior to normal retirement age ................ | 85 | 80 | 83 | 89 |
| Lump-sum postretirement survivor benefits ............. | ([2]) | - | - | - |
| Lump-sum preretirement survivor benefits ............. | 2 | 2 | 1 | 2 |
| Full pension restored if spouse predeceases retiree ............................ | 17 | 13 | 19 | 19 |

[1] Provisions that restrict benefits, such as limits on the number of years of service included in benefit computations.
[2] Less than 0.5 percent.

NOTE: Where applicable, dash indicates no employees in this category, or data do not meet publication criteria.

**Table 61. Defined benefit plans:[1] Primary formula and availability of alternative formula, full-time employees, private industry, National Compensation Survey, 2000**

| Benefit formula[2] | All employees | Professional, technical, and related employees | Clerical and sales employees | Blue-collar and service employees |
|---|---|---|---|---|
| Number (in thousands) with defined benefit plan ............ | 19,225 | 5,794 | 5,179 | 8,252 |
| | Percent | | | |
| Total with defined benefit plan .. | 100 | 100 | 100 | 100 |
| Percent of terminal earnings | 48 | 47 | 48 | 50 |
| With alternative formula .... | 15 | 15 | 12 | 16 |
| Percent of career earnings ... | 13 | 12 | 19 | 10 |
| With alternative formula .... | 2 | 4 | 1 | 1 |
| Dollar amount formula .......... | 14 | 9 | 9 | 21 |
| With alternative formula .... | 1 | - | 1 | 1 |
| Percent of contribution formula ......................... | ([3]) | - | - | 1 |
| Cash account ....................... | 23 | 31 | 23 | 18 |
| With alternative formula .... | 6 | 6 | 5 | 7 |
| Other ................................... | 1 | 1 | 2 | 1 |

[1] Cash balance retirement plans are a defined benefit plan in which an account is maintained for each participant, with employer contributions based on employee earnings, plus interest, being credited to that account. Cash balance plans generally do not have provisions for many of the features found in traditional defined benefit plans. Due to the increase in the incidence of cash balance plans, the prevalence of some defined benefit plan provisions has declined from earlier surveys.
[2] Alternative formulas are generally designed to provide a minimum benefit for employees with short service or low earnings.
[3] Less than 0.5 percent.

NOTE: Because of rounding, sums of individual items may not equal totals. Where applicable, dash indicates no employees in this category, or do not meet publication criteria.

**Table 62. Defined benefit plans: Terminal earnings formulas, full-time employees, private industry, National Compensation Survey, 2000**

| Terminal earnings | All employees | Professional, technical, and related employees | Clerical and sales employees | Blue-collar and service employees |
|---|---|---|---|---|
| Number (in thousands) with terminal earnings formula ... | 9,278 | 2,705 | 2,469 | 4,104 |
| | Percent | | | |
| Total with terminal earnings formula ................................ | 100 | 100 | 100 | 100 |
| Flat percent per year of service ........................... | 34 | 38 | 37 | 31 |
| Percent per year varies ........ | 62 | 59 | 63 | 63 |
| By service ......................... | 14 | 16 | 13 | 12 |
| By earnings ....................... | 35 | 30 | 36 | 38 |
| By earnings and service ... | 13 | 13 | 14 | 12 |
| Other ...................................... | 4 | 3 | ([1]) | 6 |

[1] Less than 0.5 percent.

NOTE: Because of rounding, sums of individual items may not equal totals. Where applicable, dash indicates no employees in this category, or data do not meet publication criteria.

**Table 63. Defined benefit plans: Definition of terminal earnings, full-time employees, private industry, National Compensation Survey, 2000**

| Period of terminal earnings | All employees | Professional, technical, and related employees | Clerical and sales employees | Blue-collar and service employees |
|---|---|---|---|---|
| Number (in thousands) with terminal earnings formula ... | 9,278 | 2,705 | 2,469 | 4,104 |
| | Percent | | | |
| Total with terminal earnings formula ................................ | 100 | 100 | 100 | 100 |
| One year ............................... | 1 | ([1]) | 1 | 1 |
| Three years .......................... | 13 | 16 | 15 | 10 |
| Five years ............................ | 82 | 79 | 82 | 83 |
| Other period[2] ...................... | 5 | 5 | 3 | 6 |

[1] Less than 0.5 percent.
[2] Formulas based on earnings during period other than 3 or 5 years' service, or period not immediately before retirement (for example, first 5 of last 10 years' service).

NOTE: Because of rounding, sums of individual items may not equal totals. Where applicable, dash indicates no employees in this category, or data do not meet publication criteria.

**Table 64. Defined benefit plans: Types of earnings included in earnings-based formulas, full-time employees, private industry, National Compensation Survey, 2000**

| Type of earnings | All employees | Professional, technical, and related employees | Clerical and sales employees | Blue-collar and service employees |
|---|---|---|---|---|
| Number (in thousands) with earnings-based formula ...... | 11,778 | 3,408 | 3,451 | 4,919 |
| | Percent | | | |
| Total with earnings-based formula ................. | 100 | 100 | 100 | 100 |
| Straight-time earnings only ... | 45 | 56 | 33 | 47 |
| Straight-time earnings plus other earnings ................. | 55 | 44 | 67 | 53 |
| Overtime ................... | 42 | 37 | 44 | 43 |
| Shift differentials ............... | 20 | 18 | 19 | 21 |
| Commissions ................... | 31 | 19 | 49 | 25 |

NOTE: Sums of individual items may be greater than totals because more than one type of earnings may be included in this definition. Where applicable, dash indicates no employees in this category, or data do not meet publication criteria.

**Table 65. Defined benefit plans:[1] Integration with Social Security, full-time employees, private industry, National Compensation Survey, 2000**

| Intregration with Social Security | All employees | Professional, technical, and related employees | Clerical and sales employees | Blue-collar and service employees |
|---|---|---|---|---|
| Number (in thousands) with defined benefit pension ...... | 19,225 | 5,794 | 5,179 | 8,252 |
| | Percent | | | |
| Total with defined benefit pension ..................... | 100 | 100 | 100 | 100 |
| With integrated formula ........ | 41 | 35 | 49 | 40 |
| Step-rate excess[2] ............ | 32 | 27 | 40 | 31 |
| Social Security breakpoint ............... | 29 | 24 | 38 | 25 |
| Dollar amount breakpoint .............. | 3 | 2 | 2 | 5 |
| Offset by Social Security[3] | 9 | 9 | 9 | 10 |
| Without integrated formula ... | 59 | 65 | 51 | 60 |

[1] Cash balance retirement plans are a defined benefit plan in which an account is maintained for each participant, with employer contributions based on employee earnings, plus interest, being credited to that account. Cash balance plans generally do not have provisions for many of the features found in traditional defined benefit plans. Due to the increase in the incidence of cash balance plans, the prevalence of some defined benefit plan provisions has declined from earlier surveys.

[2] Formula applies lower benefit rate to earnings subject to FICA (Social Security) taxes or below a specific dollar breakpoint.

[3] Benefit as calculated by formula is reduced by portion of primary Social Security payments, for example, 50 percent.

NOTE: Because of rounding, sums of individual items may not equal totals. Where applicable, dash indicates no employees in this category, or data do not meet publication criteria.

**Table 66. Defined benefit plans: Maximum benefit provisions, full-time employees, private industry, National Compensation Survey, 2000**

| Maximum benefit[1] | All employees[2] |
|---|---|
| Number (in thousands) with defined benefit plan ............ | 19,225 |
| | Percent |
| Total with defined benefit plan .. | 100 |
| Subject to maximum ............. | 35 |
| Limit on years of credited service ........................ | 34 |
| Less than 30 ................. | 6 |
| 30 ................................ | 9 |
| 31 - 34 .......................... | 1 |
| 35 ................................ | 9 |
| 40 ................................ | 8 |
| Greater than 40 ........... | 2 |
| Other maximum[3] ............. | 1 |
| Not subject to maximum ....... | 65 |
| | Average[4] |
| Average credited service maximum (in years) ............ | 33.3 |

[1] These maximum provisions are independent of Internal Revenue Code ceilings on pensions payable from defined benefit plans.
[2] Data for professional, technical, and related employees, clerical and sales employees, and blue-collar and service employees were not publishable this year due to a high nonresponse rate.
[3] The benefit yielded under the formula is limited to a percent of terminal earnings or to a flat dollar amount.
[4] The average is presented for all covered workers; averages exclude workers without the plan provision.

NOTE: Sums of individual items may not equal totals because some benefit formulas contain a limit on years of credited service and another maximum provision. Where applicable, dash indicates no employees in this category, or data do not meet publication criteria.

**Table 67. Defined benefit plans: Postretirement survivor benefits, full-time employees, private industry, National Compensation Survey, 2000**

| Survivor benefit provisions | All employees | Professional, technical, and related employees | Clerical and sales employees | Blue-collar and service employees |
|---|---|---|---|---|
| Number (in thousands) with defined benefit plan ............ | 19,225 | 5,794 | 5,179 | 8,252 |
| | Percent | | | |
| Total with defined benefit plan .. | 100 | 100 | 100 | 100 |
| With postretirement survivor benefits ........................ | 99 | 100 | 99 | 99 |
| Joint and survivor annuity[1] | 99 | 100 | 99 | 99 |
| 50 percent only ............. | 15 | 16 | 19 | 13 |
| 51 - 99 percent only ...... | 4 | 1 | 2 | 7 |
| Retiree choice of percentages ............ | 76 | 76 | 77 | 76 |
| Highest: | | | | |
| 50 percent ............ | 1 | 2 | ([2]) | ([2]) |
| 51 - 99 percent ..... | 4 | 5 | ([2]) | 5 |
| 100 percent ........... | 72 | 69 | 76 | 70 |
| Not determinable .......... | 4 | 8 | 1 | 4 |
| Not determinable .................. | 1 | - | 1 | 1 |

[1] An annuity that provides income during the lifetime of both the retiree and the surviving spouse. The accrued pension will usually be actuarially reduced at retirement because of the longer time that payments are expected to be made. Employees and their spouses are required to waive the spouse annuity in writing if they desire a pension during the employee's lifetime only or another option offered by the plan, such as guarantee of payment for a specified period.
[2] Less than 0.5 percent.

NOTE: Because of rounding, sums of individual items may not equal totals. Where applicable, dash indicates no employees in this category, or data do not meet publication criteria.

**Table 68. Defined benefit plans:[1] Preretirement survivor benefits, full-time employees, private industry, National Compensation Survey, 2000**

| Survivor benefit provisions | All employees | Professional, technical, and related employees | Clerical and sales employees | Blue-collar and service employees |
|---|---|---|---|---|
| Number (in thousands) with defined benefit plan ............ | 19,225 | 5,794 | 5,179 | 8,252 |
| | Percent | | | |
| Total with defined benefit plan .. | 100 | 100 | 100 | 100 |
| With preretirement survivor benefits[2] ......................... | 95 | 95 | 99 | 93 |
| Equivalent to joint-and-survivor annuity[3] ..................... | 84 | 79 | 87 | 86 |
| 50 percent of employee's pension | 71 | 61 | 77 | 75 |
| With additional employee cost[5] ... | 1 | (4) | (4) | 3 |
| Other percent of employee's pension[6] ................. | 2 | 1 | 1 | 3 |
| Employee choice of percent .................... | 7 | 9 | 7 | 5 |
| With additional employee cost[5] ... | 1 | 2 | (4) | 1 |
| Not determinable .......... | 4 | 8 | 2 | 3 |
| Percent of accrued benefits ....................... | 9 | 14 | 8 | 5 |
| Other[7] ......................... | 2 | 1 | 3 | 2 |
| No preretirement survivor benefits ........................ | 5 | 5 | 1 | 7 |

[1] Cash balance retirement plans are a defined benefit plan in which an account is maintained for each participant, with employer contributions based on employee earnings, plus interest, being credited to that account. Cash balance plans generally do not have provisions for many of the features found in traditional defined benefit plans. Due to the increase in the incidence of cash balance plans, the prevalence of some defined benefit plan provisions has declined from earlier surveys.

[2] Survivor annuity is based upon the benefit the employee would have received if retirement had occurred on the date of death.

[3] The spouse annuity is computed as if the employee had retired with a joint-and-survivor annuity. That is, the accrued pension is first reduced because of the longer time that payments were expected to be made to both the retiree and the surviving spouse. The spouse's share is then the specified percent of the reduced amount.

[4] Less than 0.5 percent.

[5] Plan reduces the accrued employee pension benefit for each year survivor protection is in force.

[6] Other percentages range from 51 to 100 percent of retiree's pension.

[7] Includes annuity based on a dollar amount formula or percent of earnings.

NOTE: Because of rounding, sums of individual items may not equal totals. Where applicable, dash indicates no employees in this category, or data do not meet publication criteria.

**Table 69. Defined benefit plans:[1] Requirements for normal retirement, full-time employees, private industry, National Compensation Survey, 2000**

| Selected requirements for normal retirement[2] | All employees | Professional, technical, and related employees | Clerical and sales employees | Blue-collar and service employees |
|---|---|---|---|---|
| Number (in thousands) with defined benefit plan ............ | 19,225 | 5,794 | 5,179 | 8,252 |
| | Percent | | | |
| Total with defined benefit plan .. | 100 | 100 | 100 | 100 |
| No age requirement ................... | 11 | 15 | 10 | 8 |
| Less than 20 years of service | 5 | 11 | 3 | 1 |
| 30 years of service .............. | 6 | 4 | 7 | 7 |
| At age 55 ................................. | 4 | 5 | 7 | 2 |
| No service requirement ........ | 1 | 1 | 2 | (3) |
| 1 - 29 years of service .......... | 3 | 4 | 5 | 1 |
| 30 years of service .............. | (3) | - | - | 1 |
| At age 60 ................................. | 10 | 16 | 7 | 8 |
| No service requirement ........ | 2 | 2 | 2 | 2 |
| 1 - 29 years of service .......... | 8 | 15 | 5 | 5 |
| At age 62 ................................. | 21 | 18 | 16 | 26 |
| No service requirement ........ | 1 | 1 | 2 | 1 |
| 5 years of service ................. | 7 | 7 | 4 | 9 |
| 10 years of service .............. | 11 | 7 | 9 | 14 |
| 20 years of service .............. | (3) | (3) | (3) | (3) |
| At age 65 ................................. | 49 | 41 | 55 | 51 |
| No service requirement ........ | 30 | 24 | 39 | 29 |
| 5 years of service ................. | 15 | 12 | 15 | 17 |
| 10 years of service .............. | 2 | 4 | (3) | 3 |
| Sum of age plus service[4] ......... | 3 | 4 | 5 | 2 |
| Equals less than 80 .............. | 1 | (3) | 2 | 1 |
| Equals 81 - 89 ...................... | 2 | 3 | 2 | 2 |

[1] Cash balance retirement plans are a defined benefit plan in which an account is maintained for each participant, with employer contributions based on employee earnings, plus interest, being credited to that account. Cash balance plans generally do not have provisions for many of the features found in traditional defined benefit plans. Due to the increase in the incidence of cash balance plans, the prevalence of some defined benefit plan provisions has declined from earlier surveys.

[2] Normal retirement is defined as the point at which the participant could retire and immediately receive all accrued benefits by virtue of service and earnings, without reduction due to age. If a plan had alternative age and service requirements, the earliest age and associated service were tabulated; if one alternative did not specify an age, it was the requirement tabulated. Some age and service requirements are not shown separately.

[3] Less than 0.5 percent.

[4] In some plans, participants must also satisfy a minimum age or service requirement.

NOTE: Because of rounding and because some age and service requirements are not shown separately, sums of individual items may not equal totals. Where applicable, dash indicates no employees in this category, or data do not meet publication criteria.

**Table 70. Defined benefit plans:[1] Requirements for early retirement, full-time employees, private industry, National Compensation Survey, 2000**

| Selected requirements for early retirement[2] | All employees | Professional, technical, and related employees | Clerical and sales employees | Blue-collar and service employees |
|---|---|---|---|---|
| Number (in thousands) with defined benefit plan ............... | 19,225 | 5,794 | 5,179 | 8,252 |
| | Percent | | | |
| Total with defined benefit plan ...... | 100 | 100 | 100 | 100 |
| With early retirement available ..... | 77 | 69 | 78 | 81 |
| No age requirement ................... | 10 | 5 | 5 | 16 |
| 30 years of service .............. | 7 | 5 | 4 | 11 |
| Less than age 55 ................... | 9 | 9 | 13 | 7 |
| No service requirement[4] ....... | (3) | (3) | - | - |
| 5 years of service ................ | 2 | 1 | 3 | 2 |
| 10 years of service .............. | 3 | 4 | 4 | 2 |
| 15 years of service .............. | 2 | 3 | 2 | 1 |
| 25 years of service .............. | 2 | 2 | 4 | 1 |
| At age 55 ......................... | 50 | 45 | 55 | 49 |
| No service requirement[4] ....... | 1 | 3 | 1 | 1 |
| 5 years of service ................ | 29 | 26 | 30 | 29 |
| 10 years of service .............. | 13 | 10 | 18 | 11 |
| 15 years of service .............. | 6 | 4 | 6 | 7 |
| At age 60 ......................... | 2 | 3 | 1 | 1 |
| At age 62 ......................... | 1 | - | - | 2 |
| Early retirement not available ....... | 23 | 31 | 22 | 19 |

[1] Cash balance retirement plans are a defined benefit plan in which an account is maintained for each participant, with employer contributions based on employee earnings, plus interest, being credited to that account. Cash balance plans generally do not have provisions for many of the features found in traditional defined benefit plans. Due to the increase in the incidence of cash balance plans, the prevalence of some defined benefit plan provisions has declined from earlier surveys.

[2] Early retirement is defined as the point at which a worker could retire and immediately receive accrued benefits based on service and earnings but reduced for each year prior to normal retirement age. If a plan had alternative age and service requirements, the earliest age and associated service were tabulated; if one alternative did not specify an age, it was the requirement tabulated. Many age and service breaks are not shown separately.

[3] Less than 0.5 percent.

[4] Where no service requirement is specified for early retirement, the service required for full vesting, usually 5 years, applies.

NOTE: Because of rounding and because many age and service breaks are not shown separately, sums of individual items may not equal totals. Where applicable, dash indicates no employees in this category, or data do not meet publication criteria.

**Table 71. Defined benefit plans: Early retirement reduction, full-time employees, private industry, National Compensation Survey, 2000**

| Early retirement reduction[1] | All employees | Professional, technical, and related employees | Clerical and sales employees | Blue-collar and service employees |
|---|---|---|---|---|
| Number (in thousands) with early retirement available ... | 14,729 | 3,974 | 4,042 | 6,714 |
| | Percent | | | |
| Total with early retirement available ............................ | 100 | 100 | 100 | 100 |
| Uniform percentage reduction[2] ....................... | 31 | 27 | 35 | 31 |
| Reduction varies ................... | 57 | 53 | 59 | 58 |
| By service ....................... | 2 | 3 | (3) | 3 |
| By age ........................... | 55 | 50 | 59 | 56 |
| Reduction differs each year[4] ........................ | 31 | 26 | 38 | 30 |
| Reduction differs by age bracket[5] ..................... | 24 | 24 | 21 | 25 |
| Other reduction[6] ................... | 8 | 9 | 5 | 9 |
| Not determinable ................. | 4 | 11 | 1 | 2 |

[1] Reduction for each year prior to normal retirement.

[2] In specific cases, uniform percentage reductions may approximate actuarial reductions, such as early retirement at age 55 with a reduction of 6 percent per year between age 55 and the plan's normal retirement age of 62.

[3] Less than 0.5 percent.

[4] Reduction schedule is related to actuarial assumptions of the life expectancy at age that pension payments begin.

[5] Rate of reduction is held constant within age brackets, but differs among brackets, sometimes in approximation of an actuarial table. For example, benefits may be reduced by 6 percent for each year between age 60 and the plan's normal retirement age, and by 3 percent for each year retirement precedes age 60. Also includes some plans that reduce benefits arithmetically for each year immediately below normal retirement age and actuarially below a specified age, usually 55.

[6] Reduced amount was not derived from normal retirement formula.

NOTE: Because of rounding, sums of individual items may not equal totals. Where applicable, dash indicates no employees in this category, or data do not meet publication criteria.

**Table 72. Defined benefit plans: Method of calculating disability retirement benefits, full-time employees, private industry, National Compensation Survey, 2000**

| Benefit provisions | All employees | Professional, technical, and related employees | Clerical and sales employees | Blue-collar and service employees |
|---|---|---|---|---|
| Number (in thousands) with defined benefit plan ............ | 19,225 | 5,794 | 5,179 | 8,252 |
| | Percent | | | |
| Total with defined benefit plan .. | 100 | 100 | 100 | 100 |
| With disability retirement available ........................ | 69 | 65 | 66 | 73 |
| Immediate disability retirement[1] ................... | 45 | 45 | 33 | 52 |
| Unreduced normal benefits[2] ................. | 25 | 27 | 20 | 27 |
| Reduced normal benefits[3] ................. | 15 | 17 | 13 | 14 |
| Other than normal benefits[4] ................. | 5 | 1 | 1 | 10 |
| Deferred disability retirement ................... | 24 | 20 | 33 | 22 |
| With benefits based on: | | | | |
| Service when disabled .............. | 4 | 4 | 7 | 2 |
| Service to retirement age ...................... | 20 | 16 | 26 | 20 |
| Disability retirement not available .......................... | 28 | 27 | 34 | 25 |
| Not determinable ................. | 3 | 8 | 1 | 1 |

[1] Immediate disability pensions may be supplemented by additional allowances until an employee reaches a specified age or becomes eligible for Social Security.

[2] The disabled worker's pension is computed under the plan's normal benefit formula and is paid as if retirement had occurred on the plan's normal retirement date, either based on years of service actually completed or projected to a later date.

[3] The disabled worker's pension is computed under the plan's normal benefit formula, based on years of service actually completed, and then reduced for early receipt.

[4] The disabled worker's benefit is not computed by the plan's normal benefit formula. The methods used include flat amount benefits, dollar amount formulas, percent of unreduced normal benefits less Social Security, and percent of earnings formula both with and without Social Security offsets.

NOTE: Because of rounding, sums of individual items may not equal totals. Where applicable, dash indicates no employees in this category, or data do not meet publication criteria.

**Table 73. Defined benefit plans: Requirements for disability retirement, full-time employees, private industry, National Compensation Survey, 2000**

| Requirements for disability retirement[1] | All employees | Professional, technical, and related employees | Clerical and sales employees | Blue-collar and service employees |
|---|---|---|---|---|
| Number (in thousands) with defined benefit plan ............ | 19,225 | 5,794 | 5,179 | 8,252 |
| | Percent | | | |
| Total with defined benefit plan .. | 100 | 100 | 100 | 100 |
| With disability retirement available ........................ | 69 | 65 | 66 | 73 |
| No minimum requirements | 9 | 6 | 13 | 9 |
| No age requirement .......... | 29 | 25 | 20 | 37 |
| Age and/or service requirement ............... | 35 | 31 | 23 | 44 |
| Receipt of long-term disability insurance benefits[2] ................. | 21 | 24 | 25 | 17 |
| Minimum vesting requirement[3] ............... | 3 | 4 | 3 | 3 |
| Disability retirement not available ........................ | 28 | 27 | 34 | 25 |
| Not determinable ................. | 3 | 8 | 1 | 1 |

[1] Non-occupational disability retirement is defined as the point at which participants retire due to an injury or illness before eligibility for early or normal retirement benefits.

[2] Receipt of long-term disability insurance benefits provides a monthly benefit to employees, who due to illness or injury, are unable to work for an extended period of time. Benefit payments usually begin after 3 or 6 months of disability and continue until retirement age is reached, or for a specified number of months, depending on the employee's age at the time of the disability.

[3] An employee may be entitled to pension benefits after satisfying vesting service requirements, usually 5 years.

NOTE: Because of rounding, sums of individual items may not equal totals. Where applicable, dash indicates no employees in this category, or data do not meet publication criteria.

**Table 74. Defined benefit plans: Vesting requirements, full-time employees, private industry, National Compensation Survey, 2000**

| Vesting requirements | All employ-ees[1] | Profes-sional, techni-cal, and related em-ploy-ees | Clerical and sales em-ploy-ees |
|---|---|---|---|
| Number (in thousands) with defined benefit plan ............ | 19,225 | 5,794 | 5,179 |
| | Percent | | |
| Total with defined benefit plan .. | 100 | 100 | 100 |
| Immediate full vesting ........... | ([2]) | ([2]) | - |
| Cliff vesting[3] .......................... | 93 | 97 | 93 |
| With full vesting: | | | |
| At any age ..................... | 88 | 92 | 92 |
| Less than 5 years ..... | 1 | 1 | 1 |
| 5 years ..................... | 85 | 90 | 90 |
| 10 years ................... | 1 | 1 | 1 |
| After specified age[4] ...... | 6 | 5 | 1 |
| 5 years ..................... | 6 | 5 | 1 |
| Graduated vesting[5] .............. | 7 | 3 | 7 |
| With full vesting after: | | | |
| Less than 7 years ......... | 6 | 3 | 5 |
| 7 years ......................... | 1 | - | 1 |

[1] Provisions for blue-collar and service employees were not publishable this year due to a high nonresponse rate. Data for this occupational group, however, are included in the estimates for all employees.
[2] Less than 0.5 percent.
[3] Under a cliff vesting schedule, an employee is not entitled to any benefits accrued under a pension plan until satisfying the requirement for 100-percent vesting.
[4] Sponsors may exclude years of service completed before age 18 from counting towards satisfaction of minimum vesting standards.
[5] Graduated vesting schedules give an employee rights to a gradually increasing share of pension benefits determined by years of service, eventually reaching 100-percent vesting status.

NOTE: Because of rounding, sums of individual items may not equal totals. Where applicable, dash indicates no employees in this category, or data do not meet publication criteria.

**Table 75. Defined benefit plans: Eligibility requirements, full-time employees, private industry, National Compensation Survey, 2000**

| Eligibility requirements[1] | All em-ploy-ees | Profes-sional, techni-cal, and related em-ploy-ees | Clerical and sales em-ploy-ees | Blue-collar and service em-ploy-ees |
|---|---|---|---|---|
| Number (in thousands) with defined benefit plan ............ | 19,225 | 5,794 | 5,179 | 8,252 |
| | Percent | | | |
| Total with defined benefit plan .. | 100 | 100 | 100 | 100 |
| Plan participation available to new employees ............... | 100 | 100 | 100 | 100 |
| With minimum age and/or service requirement[2] ..... | 74 | 72 | 85 | 68 |
| Service requirement only .. | 29 | 34 | 24 | 28 |
| Less than 1 year ........... | 5 | 6 | 6 | 4 |
| 1 year ........................ | 23 | 28 | 17 | 24 |
| More than 1 year ......... | 1 | - | 1 | 1 |
| Age 21 requirement[3] ........ | 44 | 37 | 61 | 38 |
| No service .................... | 6 | 5 | 3 | 8 |
| 1 year ...................... | 37 | 30 | 56 | 30 |
| No minimum age or service requirement ................... | 26 | 28 | 15 | 32 |
| | Average[4] | | | |
| Average service requirement (in months) ............................. | 11.8 | 11.3 | 11.7 | 12.1 |

[1] Excludes administrative time lags.
[2] May include other age and/or service requirements not shown separately
[3] The Internal Revenue Code requires that nearly all plans must allow participation to full-time employees who have reached the age of 21 and who have completed one year of service. Plans that provide immediate vesting of accrued benefits may require up to three years. Church plans are exempt from the Internal Revenue Code.
[4] The average is presented for all covered workers; averages exclude workers without the plan provision.

NOTE: Because of rounding, sums of individual items may not equal totals. Where applicable, dash indicates no employees in this category, or data do not meet publication criteria.

**Table 76. Defined benefit plans:[1] Availability of lump sum benefits at retirement, full-time employees, private industry, National Compensation Survey, 2000**

| Option | All employees | Professional, technical, and related employees | Clerical and sales employees | Blue-collar and service employees |
|---|---|---|---|---|
| Number (in thousands) with defined benefit plan ............ | 19,225 | 5,794 | 5,179 | 8,252 |
| | Percent | | | |
| Total with defined benefit plan .. | 100 | 100 | 100 | 100 |
| With lump sum available ....... | 43 | 44 | 51 | 37 |
| Full lump sum available .... | 42 | 43 | 49 | 36 |
| Limited to specified amount[2] .................. | 4 | 4 | 6 | 3 |
| No limit .......................... | 37 | 39 | 43 | 33 |
| Partial lump sum with reduced annuity .......... | 1 | 1 | 2 | 1 |
| No lump sum available ........ | 53 | 47 | 46 | 61 |
| Not determinable ................. | 4 | 8 | 3 | 2 |

[1] Cash balance retirement plans are a defined benefit plan in which an account is maintained for each participant, with employer contributions based on a percentage of employee earnings, plus interest, being credited to that account. Cash balance plans generally provide for a lump-sum payment option at retirement usually not found in traditional defined benefit plans. Due to the increase in the incidence of cash balance plans, the prevalence of some defined benefit plan provisions has declined from earlier surveys.
[2] Plan allows a full lump sum up to a maximum dollar amount.

NOTE: Because of rounding, sums of individual items may not equal totals. Where applicable, dash indicates no employees in this category, or data do not meet publication criteria.

**Table 77. Savings and thrift plans: Summary of provisions, full-time employees, private industry, National Compensation Survey, 2000**

| Item | All em-ploy-ees | Profes-sional, techni-cal, and related em-ploy-ees | Clerical and sales em-ploy-ees | Blue-collar and service em-ploy-ees |
|---|---|---|---|---|
| Number (in thousands) with savings and thrift plans ....... | 26,903 | 8,920 | 7,896 | 10,088 |
| Percent | | | | |
| Total with savings and thrift plans .................. | 100 | 100 | 100 | 100 |
| Pre-tax contributions allowed | 99 | 99 | 99 | 100 |
| Transfer/rollover contributions allowed ...... | 72 | 74 | 71 | 71 |
| Employee choice of investments for employee contributions ................... | 91 | 91 | 91 | 92 |
| Employee choice of investments for employer contributions ................... | 65 | 67 | 63 | 64 |
| Immediate full vesting .......... | 25 | 25 | 20 | 28 |
| Withdrawals permitted .......... | 50 | 48 | 47 | 54 |

NOTE: Because of rounding, sums of individual items may not equal totals. Where applicable, dash indicates no employees in this category, or data do not meet publication criteria.

**Table 78. Savings and thrift plans: Transfer and rollover provisions,[1] full-time employees, private industry, National Compensation Survey, 2000**

| Item | All em-ploy-ees | Profes-sional, techni-cal, and related em-ploy-ees | Clerical and sales em-ploy-ees | Blue-collar and service em-ploy-ees |
|---|---|---|---|---|
| Number (in thousands) with savings and thrift plans ....... | 26,903 | 8,920 | 7,896 | 10,088 |
| Percent | | | | |
| Total with savings and thrift plans .................. | 100 | 100 | 100 | 100 |
| Transfers/rollovers allowed ... | 72 | 74 | 71 | 71 |
| Transfers/rollovers not allowed .......................... | 22 | 20 | 23 | 22 |
| Not determinable ................. | 6 | 6 | 6 | 7 |

[1] Participants are allowed to transfer/rollover contributions and earnings from a previous employer's plan.

NOTE: Because of rounding, sums of individual items may not equal totals. Where applicable, dash indicates no employees in this category, or data do not meet publication criteria.

**Table 79. Savings and thrift plans: Maximum employee contributions,[1] full-time employees, private industry, National Compensation Survey, 2000**

| Maximum employee contributions | All employees[2] | Professional, technical, and related employees | Clerical and sales employees |
|---|---|---|---|
| Number (in thousands) with savings and thrift plans ....... | 26,903 | 8,920 | 7,896 |
| | Percent | | |
| Total with savings and thrift plans ................................. | 100 | 100 | 100 |
| Percent of employee earnings ......................... | 90 | 89 | 91 |
| 5 percent or less ............... | ([3]) | 1 | ([3]) |
| 6 percent .......................... | 1 | 1 | ([3]) |
| 8 percent .......................... | ([3]) | ([3]) | ([3]) |
| 10 percent ........................ | 5 | 8 | 7 |
| 12 percent ........................ | 4 | 6 | 5 |
| 13 percent ........................ | ([3]) | ([3]) | ([3]) |
| 14 percent ........................ | 2 | ([3]) | 1 |
| 15 percent ........................ | 37 | 33 | 34 |
| 16 percent ........................ | 16 | 17 | 19 |
| 17 percent ........................ | 6 | 6 | 5 |
| 18 percent ........................ | 4 | 4 | 3 |
| 19 percent ........................ | ([3]) | ([3]) | ([3]) |
| 20 percent ........................ | 9 | 10 | 9 |
| 20.01 - 24.99 percent ....... | 3 | 2 | 6 |
| 25 percent or more .......... | 2 | 1 | 1 |
| Specified dollar amount ........ | 1 | 1 | 1 |
| Up to the Internal Revenue Code limit ...................... | 9 | 10 | 9 |
| | Average[4] | | |
| Average maximum contribution (percent of earnings) .......... | 15.8 | 15.4 | 15.8 |

**Table 80. Savings and thrift plans: Method of determining pretax contributions, full-time employees, private industry, National Compensation Survey, 2000**

| Pretax contributions | All employees[1] |
|---|---|
| Number (in thousands) with savings and thrift plans ....... | 26,903 |
| | Percent |
| Total with savings and thrift plans ................................. | 100 |
| Pretax contributions allowed | 99 |
| All contributions [2] ............. | 91 |
| Some Contributions .......... | 8 |
| Pretax contributions not allowed ......................... | - |
| Not determinable ................... | 1 |

[1] Provisions for professional, technical, and related employees, clerical and sales emloyees, and blue-collar and service employees were not publishable this year due to a high nonresponse rate. Data for these occupational groups, however, are included in the estimates for all employees.
[2] The plan documents specify that all contributions must or may be pretax.

NOTE: Because of rounding, sums of individual items may not equal totals. Where applicable, dash indicates no employees in this category, or data do not meet publication criteria.

[1] Includes contributions that are not matched by the employer. If maximum contributions vary, such as by length of service, the highest possible contribution was tabulated.
[2] Provisions for blue-collar and service employees were not publishable this year due to a high nonresponse rate. Data for this occupational group, however, are Included in the estimates for all employees.
[3] Less than 0.5 percent.
[4] The average is presented for all covered workers; averages exclude workers without the plan provision.

NOTE: Because of rounding, sums of individual items may not equal totals. Where applicable, dash indicates no employees in this category, or data do not meet publication criteria.

**Table 81.  Savings and thrift plans:  Maximum pretax employee contributions,[1] full-time employees, private industry, National Compensation Survey, 2000**

| Maximum pretax contributions | All employees[2] | Professional, technical, and related employees | Clerical and sales employees |
|---|---|---|---|
| Number (in thousands) with savings and thrift plans that allow pretax contributions ... | 26,705 | 8,842 | 7,822 |
| | Percent | | |
| Total with savings and thrift plans that allow pretax contributions ........................ | 100 | 100 | 100 |
| Percent of employee earnings ......................... | 90 | 89 | 91 |
| 5 percent or less .............. | ([3]) | 1 | ([3]) |
| 6 percent ........................... | 1 | 1 | ([3]) |
| 8 percent ........................... | ([3]) | ([3]) | ([3]) |
| 10 percent ......................... | 7 | 9 | 9 |
| 12 percent ......................... | 4 | 6 | 5 |
| 13 percent ......................... | ([3]) | ([3]) | ([3]) |
| 14 percent ......................... | 2 | ([3]) | 1 |
| 15 percent ......................... | 38 | 34 | 35 |
| 16 percent ......................... | 19 | 20 | 22 |
| 17 percent ......................... | 2 | 2 | 3 |
| 18 percent ......................... | 3 | 3 | 2 |
| 19 percent ......................... | ([3]) | ([3]) | ([3]) |
| 20 percent ......................... | 7 | 8 | 6 |
| 20.01 - 24.99 percent ....... | 3 | 1 | 6 |
| 25 percent or more ........... | 2 | 1 | 1 |
| Not determinable .............. | 1 | 1 | 1 |
| Specified dollar amount ........ | 1 | 1 | 1 |
| Up to the Internal Revenue Code limit ........................ | 9 | 10 | 9 |
| | Average[4] | | |
| Average maximum pretax contribution (percent of earnings ............................. | 15.6 | 15.3 | 15.5 |

**Table 82.  Savings and thrift plans:  Methods of employer matching contributions, full-time employees, private industry, National Compensation Survey, 2000**

| Employer matching rates | All employees | Professional, technical, and related employees | Clerical and sales employees | Blue-collar and service employees |
|---|---|---|---|---|
| Number (in thousands) with savings and thrift plans ....... | 26,903 | 8,920 | 7,896 | 10,088 |
| | Percent | | | |
| Total with savings and thrift plans ................................... | 100 | 100 | 100 | 100 |
| Specified matching percent[1] | 69 | 73 | 69 | 67 |
| Varies by service .................. | 4 | 4 | 4 | 5 |
| Varies by amount of contribution ...................... | 8 | 7 | 5 | 10 |
| Varies by profit level ............ | 1 | ([2]) | 1 | ([2]) |
| Other ................................... | 2 | 1 | 1 | 3 |
| Not determinable .................. | 16 | 15 | 19 | 15 |

[1]  Plans where the employer matches a specified percent of employee contributions.  For example, the employer matches 50 percent of employee earnings up to 6 percent.
[2]  Less than 0.5 percent.

NOTE:  Because of rounding, sums of individual items may not equal totals. Where applicable, dash indicates no employees in this category, or data do not meet publication criteria.

[1]  Includes contributions that are not matched by the employer. If maximum contributions vary, such as by length of service, the highest possible contribution was tabulated.
[2]  Provisions for blue-collar and service employees were not publishable this year due to a high nonresponse rate. Data for this occupational group, however, are included in the estimates for all employees.
[3]  Less than 0.5 percent.
[4]  The average is presented for all covered workers; averages exclude workers without the plan provision.

NOTE:  Because of rounding, sums of individual items may not equal totals.  Where applicable, dash indicates no employees in this category, or data do not meet publication criteria.

**Table 83. Savings and thrift plans: Employee contributions by employer specified matching percentage, full-time employees, private industry, National Compensation Survey, 2000**

| Employee contribution[1] | Total[2] | Specified matching percentage | | | |
|---|---|---|---|---|---|
| | | 1 - 49 | 50 | 51 - 99 | 100 |
| | | Percent | | | |
| **All employees[3]** | | | | | |
| Total[4] ................................... | 100 | 14 | 40 | 21 | 25 |
| Under 2 percent ............... | 1 | ([5]) | 1 | - | - |
| 2 percent ........................... | 3 | - | 1 | ([5]) | 1 |
| 3 percent ........................... | 6 | 1 | 3 | 1 | 2 |
| 4 percent ........................... | 19 | 5 | 6 | - | 8 |
| 5 percent ........................... | 15 | 1 | 2 | 4 | 7 |
| Greater than 5 percent ..... | 56 | 7 | 26 | 17 | 6 |
| **Professional, technical, and related employees** | | | | | |
| Total[4] ................................... | 100 | 16 | 38 | 18 | 28 |
| Under 2 percent ............... | 1 | 1 | ([5]) | - | - |
| 2 percent ........................... | 2 | - | ([5]) | ([5]) | 2 |
| 3 percent ........................... | 7 | 2 | 4 | ([5]) | 2 |
| 4 percent ........................... | 25 | 6 | 8 | - | 11 |
| 5 percent ........................... | 9 | ([5]) | ([5]) | ([5]) | 7 |
| Greater than 5 percent ..... | 56 | 7 | 26 | 17 | 6 |
| **Clerical and sales employees** | | | | | |
| Total[4] ................................... | 100 | 13 | 41 | 22 | 25 |
| 2 percent ........................... | 1 | - | 1 | ([5]) | 1 |
| 3 percent ........................... | 5 | ([5]) | 2 | ([5]) | 2 |
| 4 percent ........................... | 17 | 3 | 7 | - | 7 |
| 5 percent ........................... | 15 | 1 | 2 | 7 | 5 |
| Greater than 5 percent ..... | 61 | 8 | 28 | 15 | 10 |

[1] Employee may contribute a percent of salary up to a specified maximum; ceilings on contributions to be matched by employers generally are lower.

[2] Total includes workers with an employer matching percentage of greater than 100 percent, but those matching percentages are not presented separately.

[3] Provisions for blue-collar and service employees were not publishable this year due to a high nonresponse rate. Data for this occupational group, however, are included in the estimates for all employees.

[4] Includes other employee contribution rates not shown separately.

[5] Less than 0.5 percent.

NOTE: Because of rounding, sums of individual items may not equal totals. Where applicable, dash indicates no employees in this category, or data do not meet publication criteria.

**Table 84. Savings and thrift plans: Investment choices, full-time employees, private industry, National Compensation Survey, 2000**

| Investment choices | All employees | | Professional, technical, and related employees | | Clerical and sales employees | | Blue-collar and service employees | |
|---|---|---|---|---|---|---|---|---|
| | Employee contributions | Employer contributions | Employee contributions | Employer contributions | Employee contributions | Employer contributions | Employee contributions | Employer contributions |
| Number (in thousands) with savings and thrift plans ....... | 26,903 | 26,903 | 8,920 | 8,920 | 7,896 | 7,896 | 10,088 | 10,088 |
| Percent | | | | | | | | |
| Total with savings and thrift plans ................................... | 100 | 100 | 100 | 100 | 100 | 100 | 100 | 100 |
| Employee permitted to choose investments ........ | 91 | 65 | 91 | 67 | 91 | 63 | 92 | 64 |
| Two choices ...................... | 2 | 1 | 2 | 1 | 2 | ($^1$) | 2 | 1 |
| Three choices ................... | 2 | 2 | 1 | 1 | 1 | 1 | 5 | 5 |
| Four choices ..................... | 1 | 1 | 1 | ($^1$) | 1 | 1 | 1 | 1 |
| Five choices ..................... | 9 | 7 | 9 | 8 | 8 | 6 | 9 | 8 |
| Six choices ...................... | 6 | 3 | 6 | 4 | 9 | 4 | 4 | 2 |
| Seven choices .................. | 7 | 5 | 10 | 9 | 3 | 3 | 7 | 4 |
| Eight choices ................... | 5 | 1 | 2 | 1 | 7 | 2 | 6 | 2 |
| Nine choices .................... | 6 | 6 | 5 | 4 | 10 | 10 | 5 | 5 |
| Ten choices ..................... | 11 | 9 | 11 | 8 | 12 | 10 | 11 | 9 |
| More than ten choices ...... | 22 | 15 | 25 | 18 | 18 | 12 | 23 | 15 |
| Not determinable ............. | 19 | 15 | 20 | 13 | 21 | 17 | 18 | 14 |
| Employee not permitted to choose investments ........ | 5 | 31 | 6 | 30 | 5 | 32 | 3 | 32 |
| Not determinable ................... | 4 | 4 | 4 | 3 | 4 | 4 | 5 | 4 |

[1] Less than 0.5 percent.

NOTE: Because of rounding, sums of individual items may not equal totals. Where applicable, dash indicates no employees in this category, or data do not meet publication criteria.

**Table 85. Savings and thrift plans: Types of investments allowed in plans permitting employees to choose investments, full-time employees, private industry, National Compensation Survey, 2000**

| Investment | All employees | | Professional, technical, and related employees | | Clerical and sales employees | | Blue-collar and service employees | |
|---|---|---|---|---|---|---|---|---|
| | Employee contributions | Employer contributions | Employee contributions | Employer contributions | Employee contributions | Employer contributions | Employee contributions | Employer contributions |
| Number (in thousands) with savings and thrift plans ....... | 26,903 | 26,903 | 8,920 | 8,920 | 7,896 | 7,896 | 10,088 | 10,088 |
| | Percent | | | | | | | |
| Total with savings and thrift plans ................................... | 100 | 100 | 100 | 100 | 100 | 100 | 100 | 100 |
| Total with employee investment choice allowed ......................... | 91 | 65 | 91 | 67 | 91 | 63 | 92 | 64 |
| Company stock ................. | 38 | 20 | 35 | 22 | 37 | 17 | 41 | 21 |
| Common stock fund ......... | 62 | 44 | 62 | 48 | 57 | 39 | 66 | 45 |
| Long-term interest bearing securities ..................... | 59 | 42 | 57 | 45 | 56 | 38 | 62 | 43 |
| Diversified stock and bond fund ............................. | 63 | 44 | 61 | 46 | 60 | 39 | 68 | 45 |
| Government securities ...... | 12 | 7 | 11 | 7 | 11 | 6 | 14 | 8 |
| Guaranteed investment contracts .................... | 6 | 5 | 7 | 6 | 5 | 4 | 6 | 5 |
| Money market funds ......... | 32 | 22 | 28 | 21 | 36 | 25 | 32 | 20 |
| Certificates of deposit ....... | ($^1$) | ($^1$) | ($^1$) | ($^1$) | ($^1$) | ($^1$) | 1 | ($^1$) |
| Other[2] ............................. | 4 | 3 | 5 | 4 | 3 | 3 | 5 | 4 |
| Determined by trustee ...... | 1 | ($^1$) | 1 | 1 | 2 | ($^1$) | 1 | ($^1$) |
| Not determinable .............. | 22 | 18 | 23 | 17 | 24 | 21 | 20 | 16 |
| Investment choice not allowed ......................... | 5 | 31 | 6 | 30 | 5 | 32 | 3 | 32 |
| Investment choice not determinable ................... | 4 | 4 | 4 | 3 | 4 | 4 | 5 | 4 |

[1] Less than 0.5 percent.
[2] Includes purchase of life insurance, annuities, real estate, mortgage, and deposits in credit unions or savings accounts.

NOTE: Sums of individual items do not equal totals because employees are often offered a number of investment choices. Where applicable, dash indicates no employees in this category, or data do not meet publication criteria.

**Table 86. Savings and thrift plans: Frequency of investment changes, full-time employees, private industry, National Compensation Survey, 2000**

| Item | All employees[1] | | Professional, technical, and related employees | |
|---|---|---|---|---|
| | Employee contribu-tions | Employer contribu-tions | Employee contribu-tions | Employer contribu-tions |
| Number (in thousands) with savings and thrift plans ....... | 26,903 | 26,903 | 8,920 | 8,920 |
| | Percent | | | |
| Total with savings and thrift plans ................................... | 100 | 100 | 100 | 100 |
| Total with employee investment choice allowed ........................... | 91 | 65 | 91 | 67 |
| At any time ........................ | 68 | 50 | 66 | 50 |
| Specified number of times per year ....................... | 16 | 9 | 14 | 9 |
| One .............................. | (2) | (2) | (2) | (2) |
| Two .............................. | (2) | (2) | (2) | (2) |
| Four ............................. | 8 | 6 | 6 | 4 |
| Five or more ................. | 8 | 3 | 8 | 4 |
| Other ............................... | (2) | (2) | (2) | (2) |
| Not determinable ............. | 7 | 6 | 11 | 8 |
| Investment choice not allowed ........................... | 5 | 31 | 6 | 30 |
| Investment choice not determinable ................... | 4 | 4 | 4 | 3 |

[1] Provisions for clerical and sales employees and blue-collar and service employees were not publishable this year due to a high nonresponse rate. Data for these occupational groups, however, are included in the estimates for all employees.
[2] Less than 0.5 percent.

NOTE: Because of rounding, sums of individual items may not equal totals. Where applicable, dash indicates no employees in this category, or data do not meet publication criteria.

**Table 87. Savings and thrift plans: Withdrawal availability, full-time employees, private industry, National Compensation Survey, 2000**

| Withdrawal provision | All employees | Professional, technical, and related employees | Clerical and sales employees | Blue-collar and service employees |
|---|---|---|---|---|
| Number (in thousands) with savings and thrift plans ....... | 26,903 | 8,920 | 7,896 | 10,088 |
| | Percent | | | |
| Total with savings and thrift plans ...................... | 100 | 100 | 100 | 100 |
| Withdrawals permitted .......... | 50 | 48 | 47 | 54 |
| Any reason ...................... | 21 | 20 | 20 | 23 |
| Hardship reasons only[1] .... | 29 | 29 | 28 | 31 |
| Withdrawals not permitted .... | 40 | 43 | 41 | 37 |
| Not determinable ................. | 10 | 9 | 12 | 9 |

[1] Hardship reasons may include death or illness of a family member, education expenses, sudden uninsured losses, or purchase of a primary residence.

NOTE: Because of rounding, sums of individual items may not equal totals. Where applicable, dash indicates no employees in this category, or data do not meet publication criteria.

**Table 88. Savings and thrift plans: Vesting requirements, full-time employees, private industry, National Compensation Survey, 2000**

| Vesting requirements | All employees[1] |
|---|---|
| Number (in thousands) with savings and thrift plans ....... | 26,903 |
| | Percent |
| Total with with savings and thrift plans ................... | 100 |
| Immediate full vesting .......... | 25 |
| Cliff vesting[2] ....................... | 23 |
| With full vesting after: | |
| 1 - 2 years ..................... | 2 |
| 3 - 4 years ..................... | 8 |
| 5 years ......................... | 12 |
| More than 5 years ........ | 1 |
| Graduated vesting[3] .............. | 46 |
| With full vesting after: | |
| 4 years or less ............. | 14 |
| 5 years ......................... | 21 |
| 6 years ......................... | 9 |
| 7 years ......................... | 3 |
| Class year vesting[4] .............. | 1 |
| With each class vested after: | |
| 2 years ......................... | ([5]) |
| More than 3 years ........ | 1 |
| Other ................................... | 1 |
| Not determinable ................. | 4 |

[1] Provisions for professional, technical, and related employees, clerical and sales employees, and blue-collar and service employees were not publishable this year due to a high nonresponse rate. Data for these occupational groups, however, are included in the estimates for all employees.

[2] Under cliff vesting, an employee is not entitled to any benefits until satisfying requirements for 100 percent vesting.

[3] Under graduated vesting, an employee's rights to benefits increase with length of service, eventually reaching 100 percent.

[4] Under class year vesting, employee contributions for a given year (class) become nonforfeitable after meeting vesting requirements. Subsequent contributions must meet similar requirements.

[5] Less than 0.5 percent.

NOTE: Because of rounding, sums of individual items may not equal totals. Where applicable, dash indicates no employees in this category, or data do not meet publication criteria.

**Table 89. 401(k) salary reduction plans: Transfer and rollover provisions,[1] full-time employees, private industry, National Compensation Survey, 2000**

| Item | All employees | Professional, technical, and related employees | Clerical and sales employees | Blue-collar and service employees |
|---|---|---|---|---|
| Number (in thousands) with 401(k) salary reduction plans ........................... | 30,178 | 9,969 | 9,061 | 11,147 |
| | Percent | | | |
| Total with 401(k) salary reduction plans ................... | 100 | 100 | 100 | 100 |
| Transfers/rollovers allowed ... | 70 | 73 | 68 | 69 |
| Transfers/rollovers not allowed .......................... | 24 | 22 | 26 | 24 |
| Not determinable ................. | 6 | 5 | 6 | 7 |

[1] Participants are allowed to transfer/rollover contributions and earnings from a previous employer's plan.

NOTE: Because of rounding, sums of individual items may not equal totals. Where applicable, dash indicates no employees in this category, or data do not meet publication criteria.

**Table 90. 401(k) salary reduction plans: Maximum pretax employee contributions,[1] full-time employees, private industry, National Compensation Survey, 2000**

| Maximum pretax contributions | All employees | Professional, technical, and related employees | Clerical and sales employees | Blue-collar and service employees |
|---|---|---|---|---|
| Number (in thousands) with 401(k) salary reduction plans ........................... | 30,178 | 9,969 | 9,061 | 11,147 |
| | Percent | | | |
| Total with 401(k) pretax salary reduction plans ................ | 100 | 100 | 100 | 100 |
| Percent of employee earnings ......................... | 84 | 85 | 83 | 85 |
| 5 percent or less .............. | 1 | 1 | ([2]) | ([2]) |
| 6 percent ........................ | 1 | 1 | ([2]) | 1 |
| 8 percent ........................ | 1 | 2 | 1 | ([2]) |
| 10 percent ....................... | 6 | 8 | 8 | 2 |
| 12 percent ....................... | 3 | 5 | 4 | 1 |
| 13 percent ....................... | ([2]) | ([2]) | ([2]) | ([2]) |
| 14 percent ....................... | 2 | ([2]) | 1 | 4 |
| 15 percent ....................... | 37 | 34 | 34 | 42 |
| 16 percent ....................... | 17 | 18 | 19 | 15 |
| 16.01 - 16.99 percent ....... | ([2]) | ([2]) | ([2]) | - |
| 17 percent ....................... | 2 | 2 | 2 | 1 |
| 17.01 - 17.99 percent ....... | ([2]) | ([2]) | ([2]) | - |
| 18 percent ....................... | 0 | 3 | 2 | 4 |
| 19 percent ....................... | ([2]) | ([2]) | ([2]) | ([2]) |
| 20 percent ....................... | 0 | 7 | 5 | 6 |
| 20.01 - 24.99 percent ....... | 3 | 1 | 5 | 3 |
| 25 percent or more ........... | 2 | 1 | 1 | 3 |
| Specified dollar amount ........ | 1 | 1 | 1 | 1 |
| Up to the Internal Revenue Code limit ...................... | 15 | 14 | 16 | 14 |
| | Average[3] | | | |
| Average maximum pretax contribution (percent of earnings) ............................ | 15.3 | 15.0 | 15.1 | 15.7 |

[1] Includes contributions that are not matched by the employer. If maximum contributions vary, such as by length of service, the highest possible contribution was tabulated.

[2] Less than 0.5 percent.

[3] The average is presented for all covered workers; averages exclude workers without the plan provision.

NOTE: Because of rounding, sums of individual items may not equal totals. Where applicable, dash indicates no employees in this category, or data do not meet publication criteria.

**Table 91. 401(k) salary reduction plans: Investment choices, full-time employees, private industry, National Compensation Survey, 2000**

| Investment choices for employer contributions | All employees | | Professional, technical, and related employees | | Clerical and sales employees | | Blue-collar and service employees | |
|---|---|---|---|---|---|---|---|---|
| | Employee contribu-tions | Employer contribu-tions | Employee contribu-tions | Employer contribu-tions | Employee contribu-tions | Employer contribu-tions | Employee contribu-tions | Employer contribu-tions |
| Number (in thousands) with 401(k) salary reduction plans ...................... | 30,178 | 30,178 | 9,969 | 9,969 | 9,061 | 9,061 | 11,147 | 11,147 |
| | Percent | | | | | | | |
| Total with 401(k) salary reduction plans ................... | 100 | 100 | 100 | 100 | 100 | 100 | 100 | 100 |
| Employee permitted to choose investments ........ | 88 | 64 | 89 | 65 | 88 | 62 | 89 | 63 |
| Two choices ..................... | 2 | (1) | 2 | 1 | 2 | (1) | 2 | 1 |
| Three choices ................... | 2 | 2 | 1 | 1 | 1 | 1 | 4 | 4 |
| Four choices ..................... | 1 | 1 | 1 | (1) | 2 | 1 | 2 | 2 |
| Five choices ..................... | 8 | 6 | 8 | 7 | 7 | 5 | 9 | 7 |
| Six choices ...................... | 6 | 3 | 6 | 4 | 8 | 3 | 4 | 2 |
| Seven choices .................. | 6 | 5 | 9 | 8 | 3 | 2 | 6 | 4 |
| Eight choices ................... | 5 | 1 | 2 | 1 | 6 | 2 | 6 | 2 |
| Nine choices .................... | 6 | 6 | 5 | 5 | 9 | 9 | 5 | 4 |
| Ten choices ..................... | 10 | 8 | 10 | 7 | 10 | 8 | 10 | 8 |
| More than ten choices ...... | 21 | 13 | 24 | 16 | 16 | 10 | 21 | 14 |
| Not determinable .............. | 22 | 17 | 21 | 14 | 24 | 20 | 20 | 17 |
| Employee not permitted to choose investments ........ | 7 | 32 | 8 | 32 | 7 | 32 | 6 | 32 |
| Not determinable .................. | 5 | 4 | 3 | 3 | 5 | 6 | 5 | 4 |

[1] Less than 0.5 percent.

NOTE: Because of rounding, sums of individual items may not equal totals. Where applicable, dash indicates no employees in this category, or data do not meet publication criteria.

**Table 92. 401(k) salary reduction plans: Withdrawal availability, full-time employees, private industry, National Compensation Survey, 2000**

| Withdrawal provision | All employees | Professional, technical, and related employees | Clerical and sales employees | Blue-collar and service employees |
|---|---|---|---|---|
| Number (in thousands) with 401(k) salary reduction plans .................................. | 30,178 | 9,969 | 9,061 | 11,147 |
| | Percent | | | |
| Total with 401(k) salary reduction plans .................... | 100 | 100 | 100 | 100 |
| Withdrawals permitted .......... | 49 | 48 | 45 | 51 |
| Any reason ....................... | 19 | 18 | 17 | 21 |
| Hardship reasons only[1] .... | 30 | 31 | 28 | 30 |
| Withdrawals not permitted .... | 43 | 44 | 44 | 41 |
| Not determinable .................. | 9 | 8 | 10 | 8 |

[1] Hardship reasons may include death or illness of a family member, education expenses, sudden uninsured losses, or purchase of a primary residence.

NOTE: Because of rounding, sums of individual items may not equal totals. Where applicable, dash indicates no employees in this category, or data do not meet publication criteria.

**Table 93. 401(k) salary reduction plans: Vesting requirements, full-time employees, private industry, National Compensation Survey, 2000**

| Vesting requirements | All employees[1] |
|---|---|
| Number (in thousands) with 401(k) salary reduction plans ..................................... | 30,178 |
| | Percent |
| Total with 401(k) salary reduction plans ................... | 100 |
| Immediate full vesting .......... | 24 |
| Cliff vesting[2] ...................... | 24 |
| With full vesting after: | |
| 1 -2 years ...................... | 2 |
| 3 - 4 years ...................... | 8 |
| 5 years ........................... | 14 |
| More than 5 years ........ | 1 |
| Graduated vesting[3] ............. | 46 |
| With full vesting after: | |
| 4 years or less .............. | 16 |
| 5 years ........................... | 20 |
| 6 years ........................... | 8 |
| 7 years ........................... | 3 |
| Class year vesting[4] .............. | 1 |
| With each class vested after: | |
| 2 years .......................... | ([5]) |
| More than 3 years ........ | 1 |
| Other ................................... | 1 |
| Not determinable .................. | 3 |

[1] Provisions for professional, technical, and related employees, clerical and sales employees, and blue-collar and service employees were not publishable this year due to a high nonresponse rate. Data for these occupational groups, however, are included in the estimates for all employees.

[2] Under cliff vesting, an employee is not entitled to any benefits until satisfying requirements for 100 percent vesting.

[3] Under graduated vesting, an employee's rights to benefits increase with length of service, eventually reaching 100 percent.

[4] Under class year vesting, employee contributions for a given year (class) become nonforfeitable after meeting vesting requirements. Subsequent contributions must meet similar requirements.

[5] Less than 0.5 percent.

NOTE: Because of rounding, sums of individual items may not equal totals. Where applicable, dash indicates no employees in this category, or data do not meet publication criteria.

# Chapter 4. Benefits by Selected Characteristics

This chapter presents data on the frequency of employee benefits by major industry segment, union status, and full- and part-time employment. Key definitions are provided below.

## Industry

Employee benefits are presented by two major industry divisions: Goods producing and service producing.

*Goods producing.* Included are such industries as manufacturing, mining, and construction.

*Service producing.* Included are such industries as transportation, communications, electric, gas and sanitary services; wholesale trade; retail trade; finance, insurance, and real estate; and services.

## Union status

Occupations are categorized as union or nonunion at the time of data collection. To be categorized as union, an occupation must meet the following criteria: 1) A labor organization must be recognized as the bargaining agent for workers in the occupation; 2) wage and salary rates must be determined through collective bargaining or negotiations; and 3) settlement terms must be embodied in a signed, mutually binding collective bargaining agreement.

## Part-time and full-time status

Employees are classified as full-time or part-time in accordance with the practices of surveyed establishments.

**Table 94. Summary: Participation in selected employee benefit programs, full-time employees, private industry, National Compensation Survey, 2000**

(In percent)

| Benefit | All employees | Professional, technical, and related employees | Clerical and sales employees | Blue-collar and service employees |
|---|---|---|---|---|
| **Paid time off:** | | | | |
| Holidays .......................................... | 87 | 90 | 93 | 83 |
| Vacations ........................................ | 91 | 92 | 94 | 88 |
| **Disability benefits[1]:** | | | | |
| Short-term disability ...................... | 39 | 54 | 38 | 32 |
| Long-term disability insurance ....... | 31 | 56 | 34 | 17 |
| **Survivor benefits:** | | | | |
| Life insurance ............................... | 65 | 82 | 66 | 57 |
| Accidental death and | | | | |
| dismemberment ......................... | 50 | 64 | 48 | 44 |
| Survivor income benefits ............. | 2 | 3 | 3 | 2 |
| **Health care benefits:** | | | | |
| Medical care ................................. | 61 | 69 | 62 | 57 |
| Dental care ................................... | 35 | 46 | 37 | 30 |
| Vision care ................................... | 21 | 26 | 21 | 18 |
| Outpatient prescription drug | | | | |
| coverage .................................... | 59 | 66 | 59 | 55 |
| **Retirement income benefits:** | | | | |
| All retirement[2] ............................. | 55 | 70 | 59 | 46 |
| Defined benefit .............................. | 22 | 29 | 22 | 20 |
| Defined contribution[3] ................... | 42 | 57 | 48 | 31 |
| Savings and thrift ....................... | 31 | 44 | 33 | 24 |
| Deferred profit sharing .............. | 9 | 10 | 13 | 6 |
| Employee stock ownership ....... | 2 | 2 | 3 | 1 |
| Money purchase pension ......... | 4 | 6 | 6 | 3 |
| Stock bonus ............................... | (4) | (4) | (4) | (4) |
| Simplified employee pension .... | 1 | 1 | 1 | 1 |
| Cash or deferred arrangements: | | | | |
| With employer contributions ..... | 35 | 51 | 38 | 27 |
| No employer contributions ........ | 11 | 16 | 11 | 9 |

[1] The definitions for paid sick leave and short-term disability (previously sickness and accident insurance) were changed for the 1995 survey. Paid sick leave now only includes plans that either specify a maximum number of days per year or unlimited days. Short-term disability now includes all insured, self-insured, and state-mandated plans available on a per disability basis as well as the unfunded per disability plans previously reported as sick leave. Sickness and accident insurance, reported in years prior to the 1995 survey, only included insured, self-insured, and state-mandated plans providing per disability benefits at less than full pay.

[2] Includes defined benefit pension plans and defined contribution retirement plans. The total is less than the sum of the individual items because many employees participated in both types of plans.

[3] The total is less than the sum of the individual items because some employees participated in more than one type of plan.

[4] Less than 0.5 percent.

NOTE: Because of rounding, sums of individual items may not equal totals. Where applicable, dash indicates that no data were reported.

**Table 95.  Other benefits:  Eligibility for specified benefits, full-time employees, private industry, National Compensation Survey, 2000 (In percent)**

| Benefit | All employees | Profes-sional, technical, and related employees | Clerical and sales employees | Blue-collar and service employees |
|---|---|---|---|---|
| **Income continuation plans:** | | | | |
| Severance pay ...................... | 23 | 38 | 26 | 14 |
| Supplemental unemployment benefits ............................. | 1 | 1 | 1 | 2 |
| **Family benefits:** | | | | |
| Employer assistance for child care ................................... | 5 | 11 | 5 | 2 |
| Employer provided funds .. | 2 | 4 | 3 | 1 |
| On-site child care .............. | 2 | 6 | 2 | 1 |
| Off-site child care ............. | 1 | 3 | 2 | ($^1$) |
| Adoption assistance ............ | 6 | 13 | 6 | 2 |
| Long-term care insurance ..... | 8 | 15 | 8 | 5 |
| Flexible workplace ............... | 5 | 14 | 5 | 1 |
| **Health promotion programs:** | | | | |
| Wellness programs ............... | 21 | 37 | 19 | 13 |
| Fitness center ...................... | 10 | 20 | 11 | 5 |
| **Miscellaneous benefits:** | | | | |
| Job-related travel accident insurance ..... ................. | 17 | 32 | 16 | 10 |
| Nonproduction bonuses ........ | 51 | 55 | 52 | 48 |
| Subsidized commuting ......... | 3 | 6 | 4 | 2 |
| Education assistance: | | | | |
| Job-related ....................... | 44 | 66 | 44 | 33 |
| Not job-related ................. | 11 | 20 | 10 | 7 |

$^1$  Less than 0.5 percent.

NOTE:  Because of rounding, sums of individual items may not equal totals.  Where applicable, dash indicates that no data were reported.

**Table 96. Summary: Participation in selected employee benefit programs, part-time employees, private industry, National Compensation Survey, 2000**

(In percent)

| Benefit | All employees | Professional, technical, and related employees | Clerical and sales employees | Blue-collar and service employees |
|---|---|---|---|---|
| Paid time off: | | | | |
| Holidays ............................................. | 39 | 48 | 41 | 36 |
| Vacations ............................................ | 39 | 52 | 35 | 39 |
| Disability benefits[1]: | | | | |
| Short-term disability ........................ | 12 | 12 | 13 | 11 |
| Long-term disability insurance ........ | 4 | 10 | 3 | 2 |
| Survivor benefits: | | | | |
| Life insurance .............................. | 11 | 24 | 9 | 10 |
| Accidental death and dismemberment .......................... | 8 | 16 | 8 | 7 |
| Survivor income benefits .............. | 1 | - | 1 | 1 |
| Health care benefits: | | | | |
| Medical care ................................. | 13 | 28 | 12 | 12 |
| Dental care ................................... | 6 | 12 | 7 | 4 |
| Vision care ................................... | 4 | 11 | 4 | 3 |
| Outpatient prescription drug coverage ................................... | 13 | 26 | 11 | 11 |
| Retirement income benefits: | | | | |
| All retirement[2] ................................. | 18 | 32 | 18 | 15 |
| Defined benefit ............................. | 6 | 11 | 7 | 5 |
| Defined contribution[3] ..................... | 12 | 18 | 14 | 9 |
| Savings and thrift ....................... | 8 | 16 | 9 | 5 |
| Deferred profit sharing .............. | 3 | 6 | 2 | 3 |
| Employee stock ownership ....... | 2 | 1 | 2 | 2 |
| Money purchase pension ......... | 1 | 3 | 2 | 1 |
| Simplified employee pension .... | 1 | ([4]) | 1 | 1 |
| Cash or deferred arrangements: | | | | |
| With employer contributions ..... | 9 | 22 | 9 | 6 |
| No employer contributions ........ | 6 | 10 | 5 | 6 |

[1] The definitions for paid sick leave and short-term disability (previously sickness and accident insurance) were changed for the 1995 survey. Paid sick leave now only includes plans that either specify a maximum number of days per year or unlimited days. Short-term disability now includes all insured, self-insured, and state-mandated plans available on a per disability basis as well as the unfunded per disability plans previously reported as sick leave. Sickness and accident insurance, reported in years prior to the 1995 survey, only included insured, self-insured, and state-mandated plans providing per disability benefits at less than full pay.
[2] Includes defined benefit pension plans and defined contribution retirement plans. The total is less than the sum of the individual items because many employees participated in both types of plans.
[3] The total is less than the sum of the individual items because some employees participated in more than one type of plan.
[4] Less than 0.5 percent.

NOTE: Because of rounding, sums of individual items may not equal totals. Where applicable, dash indicates that no data were reported.

**Table 97. Other benefits: Eligibility for specified benefits, part-time employees, private industry, National Compensation Survey, 2000**
(In percent)

| Benefit | All employees | Professional, technical, and related employees | Clerical and sales employees | Blue-collar and service employees |
|---|---|---|---|---|
| **Income continuation plans:** | | | | |
| Severance pay ...................... | 10 | 14 | 17 | 5 |
| Supplemental unemployment | | | | |
| benefits ............................. | (¹) | 1 | 1 | - |
| **Family benefits:** | | | | |
| Employer assistance for child | | | | |
| care ................................... | 3 | 11 | 2 | 1 |
| Employer provided funds .. | 1 | 5 | 1 | (¹) |
| On-site child care .............. | 1 | 4 | 1 | 1 |
| Off-site child care .............. | 1 | 2 | 1 | (¹) |
| Adoption assistance ............ | 2 | 3 | 2 | 1 |
| Long-term care insurance ..... | 2 | 6 | 2 | 1 |
| Flexible workplace ................ | 2 | 2 | 2 | 2 |
| **Health promotion programs:** | | | | |
| Wellness programs ............... | 7 | 17 | 8 | 4 |
| Fitness center ...................... | 5 | 12 | 6 | 3 |
| **Miscellaneous benefits:** | | | | |
| Job-related travel accident | | | | |
| insurance .......................... | 9 | 13 | 13 | 5 |
| Nonproduction bonuses ........ | 36 | 33 | 31 | 39 |
| Subsidized commuting ......... | 1 | 3 | 2 | (¹) |
| Education assistance: | | | | |
| Job-related ...................... | 15 | 38 | 15 | 10 |
| Not job-related ................. | 3 | 8 | 3 | 1 |

¹ Less than 0.5 percent.

NOTE: Because of rounding, sums of individual items may not equal totals. Where applicable, dash indicates that no data were reported.

**Table 98. Percent of workers participating in selected benefits, by worker and establishment characteristics, private industry, National Compensation Survey,[1] 2000**

| Characteristics | Retirement benefits | | | Health care benefits | | |
|---|---|---|---|---|---|---|
| | All | Defined benefit | Defined contri-bution | Medical care | Dental care | Vision care |
| Total ................................ | 48 | 19 | 36 | 52 | 29 | 17 |
| **Worker characteristics:[2]** | | | | | | |
| Professional, technical, and related employees[3] ........................ | 66 | 27 | 53 | 64 | 42 | 24 |
| Clerical and sales employees[3] ........ | 50 | 18 | 40 | 50 | 30 | 17 |
| Blue-collar and service employees[3] | 39 | 17 | 27 | 47 | 24 | 15 |
| Full time ........................... | 55 | 22 | 42 | 61 | 35 | 21 |
| Part time .......................... | 18 | 6 | 12 | 13 | 6 | 4 |
| Union .............................. | 83 | 69 | 38 | 75 | 53 | 41 |
| Nonunion .......................... | 44 | 14 | 36 | 49 | 27 | 15 |
| **Establishment characteristics:** | | | | | | |
| Goods-producing ................... | 57 | – | 44 | – | 33 | 20 |
| Service-producing ................. | 45 | 18 | 33 | 48 | 28 | 17 |
| 1-99 workers ...................... | 33 | 8 | 27 | 43 | 19 | 10 |
| 100 workers or more ............... | 65 | 33 | 46 | 61 | 41 | 26 |

| Characteristics | Survivor benefits | | | Disability benefits | |
|---|---|---|---|---|---|
| | Life insurance | Accidental death and dismem-berment | Survivor income benefits | Short-term disability | Long-term disability |
| Total ................................ | 54 | 41 | 2 | 34 | 26 |
| **Worker characteristics:[2]** | | | | | |
| Professional, technical, and related employees[3] ........................ | 76 | 58 | 3 | 50 | 51 |
| Clerical and sales employees[3] ........ | 52 | 39 | 2 | 32 | 27 |
| Blue-collar and service employees[3] | 47 | 36 | 2 | 28 | 14 |
| Full time ........................... | 65 | 50 | 2 | 39 | 31 |
| Part time .......................... | 11 | 8 | 1 | 12 | 4 |
| Union .............................. | 82 | 66 | 6 | 69 | 28 |
| Nonunion .......................... | 51 | 39 | 2 | 30 | 25 |
| **Establishment characteristics:** | | | | | |
| Goods-producing ................... | 69 | 58 | 3 | 45 | 31 |
| Service-producing ................. | 50 | 36 | 2 | 30 | 24 |
| 1-99 workers ...................... | 37 | 24 | 2 | 22 | 13 |
| 100 workers or more ............... | 75 | 62 | 3 | 47 | 40 |

[1] The survey covers all 50 States and the District of Columbia. Collection was conducted between February and December 2000. The average reference period was July 2000.

[2] Employees are classified as working either a full-time or part-time schedule based on the definition used by each establishment. Union workers are those whose wages are determined through collective bargaining.

[3] A classification system including about 480 individual occupations is used to cover all workers in the civilian economy. See the Technical Note for more information.

NOTE: Because of rounding, sums of individual items may not equal totals. Where applicable, dash indicates no employees in this category or data do not meet publication criteria.

**Table 99. Percent of workers with access to selected benefits, by worker and establishment characteristics, private industry, National Compensation Survey,[1] 2000**

| Characteristics | Paid vacations | Paid holidays | Employer assistance for child care | | | | Adoption assistance | Long-term care insurance | Flexible work place |
|---|---|---|---|---|---|---|---|---|---|
| | | | Total[2] | Employer provided funds | On-site child care | Off-site child care | | | |
| Total ............................... | 80 | 77 | 4 | 2 | 2 | 1 | 5 | 7 | 5 |
| **Worker characteristics:**[3] | | | | | | | | | |
| Professional, technical, and related employees[4] ................... | 88 | 85 | 11 | 4 | 6 | 3 | 12 | 14 | 12 |
| Clerical and sales employees[4] ........ | 80 | 80 | 5 | 3 | 1 | 2 | 5 | 7 | 4 |
| Blue-collar and service employees[4] | 77 | 73 | 2 | 1 | 1 | ([5]) | 2 | 4 | 1 |
| Full time ............................ | 91 | 87 | 5 | 2 | 2 | 1 | 6 | 8 | 5 |
| Part time ........................... | 39 | 39 | 3 | 1 | 1 | 1 | 2 | 2 | 2 |
| Union ............................... | 93 | 89 | 8 | 6 | 2 | ([5]) | 5 | 15 | 3 |
| Nonunion .......................... | 79 | 76 | 4 | 2 | 2 | 1 | 5 | 6 | 5 |
| **Establishment characteristics:** | | | | | | | | | |
| Goods-producing ..................... | 89 | 89 | 2 | 1 | ([5]) | ([5]) | 6 | 5 | 4 |
| Service-producing .................... | 78 | 74 | 5 | 2 | 3 | 1 | 4 | 8 | 5 |
| 1-99 workers ....................... | 73 | 70 | 1 | ([5]) | ([5]) | 1 | 1 | 5 | 2 |
| 100 workers or more ................. | 89 | 86 | 9 | 4 | 4 | 2 | 9 | 10 | 7 |

| Characteristics | Non-wage cash payments | | | Subsidized commuting | Education assistance | | Travel accident insurance | Health promotion benefits | |
|---|---|---|---|---|---|---|---|---|---|
| | Nonproduction bonuses | Supplemental unemployment benefits | Severance pay | | Work related | Non-work related | | Wellness programs | Fitness centers |
| Total ............................... | 48 | 1 | 20 | 3 | 38 | 9 | 15 | 18 | 9 |
| **Worker characteristics:**[3] | | | | | | | | | |
| Professional, technical, and related employees[4] ................... | 52 | 1 | 35 | 6 | 62 | 19 | 30 | 35 | 19 |
| Clerical and sales employees[4] ........ | 48 | 1 | 24 | 3 | 37 | 8 | 15 | 17 | 10 |
| Blue-collar and service employees[4] | 46 | 1 | 12 | 2 | 28 | 6 | 9 | 11 | 4 |
| Full time ............................ | 51 | 1 | 23 | 3 | 44 | 11 | 17 | 21 | 10 |
| Part time ........................... | 36 | ([5]) | 10 | 1 | 15 | 3 | 9 | 7 | 5 |
| Union ............................... | 38 | 8 | 31 | 2 | 57 | 18 | 23 | 38 | 11 |
| Nonunion .......................... | 49 | ([5]) | 19 | 3 | 36 | 8 | 14 | 16 | 9 |
| **Establishment characteristics:** | | | | | | | | | |
| Goods-producing ..................... | 51 | 4 | 21 | 1 | 45 | 14 | 19 | 19 | 10 |
| Service-producing .................... | 47 | ([5]) | 20 | 4 | 36 | 8 | 14 | 17 | 9 |
| 1-99 workers ....................... | 49 | ([5]) | 11 | 2 | 26 | 3 | 5 | 6 | 4 |
| 100 workers or more ................. | 46 | 2 | 32 | 5 | 52 | 17 | 28 | 31 | 16 |

[1] The survey covers all 50 States and the District of Columbia. Collection was conducted between February and December 2000. The average reference period was July 2000.

[2] The total may be less than the sum of individual items because some employees were receiving more than one type of employer assistance for child care.

[3] Employees are classified as working either a full-time or part-time schedule based on the definition used by each establishment. Union workers are those whose wages are determined through collective bargaining.

[4] A classification system including about 480 individual occupations is used to cover all workers in the civilian economy. See the Technical Note for more information.

[5] Less than 0.5 percent.

NOTE: Because of rounding, sums of individual items may not equal totals. Where applicable, dash indicates no employees in this category or data do not meet publication criteria.

# Appendix A. Technical Note

The National Compensation Survey (NCS) benefit incidence and provisions series provides information on availability and detailed provisions of employee benefit plans. The portion of the NCS sample from which estimates on employee benefits are made covers all private-sector establishments in the United States, with the exception of farms and private households.

## Scope of survey

The 2000 NCS benefits incidence survey obtained data from 1,436 private industry establishments, representing over 107 million workers; of this number, nearly 86 million were full-time workers and the remainder--nearly 22 million--were part-time workers. (See tables A-1 and A-2). The NCS uses the establishment's definition of full- and part-time status. For purposes of this survey, an establishment is an economic unit that produces goods or services, a central administrative office, or an auxiliary unit providing support services to a company. For private industries, the establishment is usually at a single physical location.

Data in Appendix B indicate the estimated number of full- and part-time employees within the scope of the survey, the number of responding sample establishments, and the number of sampled (and responding) occupational quotes within those establishments that are actually studied for each major Industry division. Occupational quotes are narrowly defined occupations sampled within an establishment.

## Occupational groups

Narrowly defined occupations selected for study are classified into one of the following three broad occupational groups:

*Professional, technical, and related.* Includes professional, technical, executive, administrative, managerial, and related occupations.

*Clerical and sales.* Includes clerical, administrative support, and sales occupations.

*Blue-collar and service.* Includes precision production, craft, and repair occupations; machine operators and inspectors; transportation and moving occupations; handlers, equipment cleaners, helpers, and laborers; and service occupations.

Excluded from the survey are self-employed persons, proprietors, major stockholders, members of a corporate board who are not otherwise officers of the corporation, volunteers, unpaid workers, family members who are paid token wages, the permanently disabled, partners in unincorporated firms, and U.S. citizens working overseas.

## Benefit areas

BLS requests that establishments provide data for sampled occupations on work schedules and plan details in each of the following benefit areas. Paid holidays, paid vacations, short-term disability benefits, long-term disability insurance, medical care, dental care, vision care, life insurance, defined benefit pension plans, and defined contribution plans.

Data are also collected on the incidence of the following additional benefits: Severance pay, supplemental unemployment benefits, travel accident insurance, nonproduction cash bonuses, child care, adoption assistance, long-term care insurance, flexible workplace, wellness programs, fitness centers, job-related and non-job-related educational assistance, and subsidized commuting.

## Sample design and data collection

The sample for this survey was selected using a three-stage design. The first stage involved the selection of areas. The NCS sample consists of 154 metropolitan areas and non-metropolitan areas that represent the Nation's 326 metropolitan statistical areas (as defined by the Office of Management and Budget) and the remaining portions of the 50 States. Metropolitan areas are either Metropolitan Statistical Areas (MSAs) or Consolidated Metropolitan Statistical Areas (CMSAs), as defined by the Office of Management and Budget, in 1994. Nonmetropolitan areas are counties that do not fit the metropolitan area definition.

In the second stage, the sample of establishments was drawn from the sampling frame, which is comprised of State Unemployment Insurance reports from the 50 States and the District of Columbia. The sampling frame is first stratified by industry and establishment size. The number of sample establishments allocated to each stratum is approximately proportional to the stratum employment. Each sampled establishment was selected within a stratum with a probability proportional to its employment. Use of this technique means that the larger an establishment's employment, the greater its chance of selection. Weights were applied to each establishment when the data were tabulated so that each establishment represents similar units (in terms of industry and employment size) in the economy that were not selected for collection.

The third stage of sample selection was a probability sample of occupations within a sampled establishment. Identification of the occupations for which data were to be collected was a four-step process:

1. Probability-proportional-to-size selection of establishment jobs.
2. Classification of jobs into occupations based on the Census of Population system.
3. Characterization of jobs as full-time versus part-time, union versus nonunion, and time versus incentive.
4. Determination of the level of work of each job.

Bureau field economists visit or contact sampled establishments by telephone to collect data for the survey. To reduce the reporting burden, respondents are asked to provide documents describing their defined benefit pensions, defined contribution plans, and medical, dental, and vision care plans. BLS analyzes these plans in Washington to garner the required data on plan provisions.

**Data calculation**

Tabulations in this bulletin show the percent of all employees who receive specified benefits, such as paid holidays or medical care, as well as information on the provisions of many of these benefits. To present provision data, tabulations generally indicate the percent of all employees receiving a benefit (participants) who are covered by specified features. For example, a tabulation may show the percent of workers with medical care benefits who are covered by a health maintenance organization.

The majority of tables in the bulletin indicate the percent of employees covered by a particular benefit plan or provision. In addition, average benefit provisions–such as the average annual deductible in a health care plan–are presented. In some cases, tabulations indicate both the percent of employees with a given provision and the average value of that provision. For example, tabulations indicate the percent of employees in fee-for-service medical care plans who must pay selected deductibles (such as $100, $150, and $200 per year), as well as the average deductible. (All tabulations of averages include only those employees actually covered by the provision being averaged.)

Most tables in this bulletin also include the number of employees receiving the benefit. This provides the reader with additional information on the prevalence of various benefit plans and provisions.

**Survey estimation methods**

The survey design uses an estimator that assigns the inverse of each sample unit's probability of selection as a weight to

the unit's data at each of the stages of sample selection. Three weight-adjustment factors are applied to the establishment data. The first factor is introduced to account for establishment non-response, a second factor for occupational non-response, and a third poststratification factor is introduced to adjust the estimated employment totals to actual counts of the employment by industry for the survey reference date.

The general form of the estimator for a population total Y is:

$$Y = \sum_{i=1}^{n'} \frac{f2_i f1_i}{P_i} \sum_{j=1}^{o_i} \frac{Y_{ij} f_{ij}}{P_{ij}}$$

where,

$n'$ = number of responding sample establishments;

$o_i$ = occupation sample size selected from the $i^{th}$ establishment;

$Y_{ij}$ = value for the characteristics of the $j^{th}$ selected occupation in the $i^{th}$ selected establishment;

$P_i$ = the probability of including the $i^{th}$ establishment in the sample;

$P_{ij}$ = the probability of including the $j^{th}$ occupation in the sample of occupations from the $i^{th}$ establishment;

$f1_i$ = weight adjustment factor for nonresponse for the $i^{th}$ establishment;

$f_{ij}$ = weight adjustment factor for nonresponse for the $j^{th}$ occupation in the $i^{th}$ establishment;

$f2_i$ = weight adjustment factor for poststratification totals for the $i^{th}$ establishment.

Appropriate employment or establishment totals are used to calculate the proportion, mean, or percentage that is desired.

**Reliability of estimates**

The statistics in this bulletin are estimates derived from a sample of usable occupation quotes selected from the responding establishments. They are not tabulations based on data from all employees in private establishments within scope of the survey. Consequently, the data are subject to sampling and nonsampling errors.

*Sampling errors* are the differences that can arise between results derived from a sample and those computed from observations of all units in the population being studied. When probability techniques are used to select a sample, statistical measures called "standard errors" can be calculated to measure possible sampling errors. No estimates of sample error were calculated for this survey.

*Nonsampling errors* also affect survey results. They can be attributed to many sources: Inability to obtain information about all establishments in the sample; definitional difficulties; differences in the interpretation of questions; inability or unwillingness of respondents to provide correct information; mistakes in recording or coding the data; and other errors of collection, response, processing, coverage, and estimation for missing data.

Computer edits of the data and professional review of both individual and summarized data reduce the nonsampling errors in recording, coding, and processing the data. However, to the extent that the characteristics of nonrespondents are not the same as those of respondents, nonsampling errors are introduced in the development of estimates.

**Table A-1. Number of establishments and full-time occupational quotes studied and estimated number of full-time workers within scope of survey, private industry, National Compensation Survey, 2000**

| Industry division[1] | Number of establishments studied | Number of occupational quotes studied[2] | | | |
|---|---|---|---|---|---|
| | | Total | Professional, technical, and related | Clerical and sales | Blue-collar and service |
| All industries .............................. | 1,436 | 5,303 | 1,712 | 1,498 | 2,093 |
| Manufacturing ....................... | 230 | 1,167 | 384 | 171 | 612 |
| Nonmanufacturing ................ | 1,206 | 4,136 | 1,328 | 1,327 | 1,481 |
| Mining ............................... | 10 | 56 | 20 | 15 | 21 |
| Construction ...................... | 103 | 326 | 37 | 46 | 243 |
| Transportation, communications, electric, gas, and sanitary services ......... | 108 | 434 | 132 | 127 | 175 |
| Wholesale trade ................ | 98 | 365 | 80 | 155 | 130 |
| Retail trade ....................... | 210 | 467 | 38 | 211 | 218 |
| Finance, insurance, and real estate ................... | 204 | 736 | 256 | 382 | 98 |
| Services ............................ | 473 | 1,752 | 765 | 391 | 596 |
| | | Estimated number of full-time workers within scope of survey | | | |
| All industries .............................. | | 85,939,757 | 20,138,724 | 23,915,459 | 41,885,575 |
| Manufacturing ....................... | | 17,615,070 | 4,203,918 | 2,247,392 | 11,163,761 |
| Nonmanufacturing ................ | | 68,324,687 | 15,934,806 | 21,668,068 | 30,721,814 |
| Mining ............................... | | 529,374 | 108,851 | 103,727 | 316,796 |
| Construction ...................... | | 6,739,146 | 859,881 | 810,444 | 5,068,821 |
| Transportation, communications, electric, gas, and sanitary services ......... | | 5,645,304 | 1,081,902 | 1,690,055 | 2,873,347 |
| Wholesale trade ................ | | 6,397,563 | 949,322 | 2,870,686 | 2,577,556 |
| Retail trade ....................... | | 13,399,681 | 789,083 | 4,892,649 | 7,717,949 |
| Finance, insurance, and real estate ................... | | 6,726,927 | 2,354,808 | 3,628,647 | 743,472 |
| Services ............................ | | 28,886,692 | 9,790,958 | 7,671,859 | 11,423,874 |

[1] As defined in the 1987 edition of the *Standard Industrial Classification Manual,* U.S. Office of Management and Budget. Industry data are shown for informational purposes only and are subject to larger than normal sample error. See section on reliability of estimates.

[2] These figures refer to all respondents to the survey, whether or not they provided data for all items studied. See the section on survey response.

NOTE: Because of rounding, sums of individual items may not equal totals. Where applicable, dash indicates no employees in this category, or data do not meet publication criteria.

# Appendix B.  Survey Response

## Survey response

Data for the 2000 National Compensation Survey benefits series were collected from February to December, reflecting an average reference period of July. Respondents were asked for information as of the time of data collection contact.

The following summary is a composite of establishment responses to the survey:

| Establishments | Number |
| --- | --- |
| In sample: | 2,763 |
| Out of business and out of scope | 368 |
| Refusing to respond | 914 |
| Responding fully or partially | 1,436 |

The responding establishments yielded 5,303 occupational observations (quotes) for which data were collected.

There were four procedures used to adjust for missing data from partial and full refusals. First, imputations for the number of plan participants are made for cases in which this number is not reported (approximately 35 percent of participants in medical plans, 36 percent in retirement plans, and about 15 percent of participants in all other types of plans).

Each of these participant values is imputed by selecting a similar plan from another establishment.

Second, imputations for plan provisions were made when they are not available in a responding establishment. These plan provisions are imputed by selecting a plan from another establishment with similar characteristics. Provisions from this selected plan are then used to represent the missing data.

For establishments that refuse, or are unable to provide the minimum amount of usable data, a weight adjustment is made using the sample unit employment. This technique assumes that the mean value of the nonrespondents equals the mean value of the respondents at some "detailed" cell level. These cells are defined in a manner that groups establishments together that are homogeneous with respect to the characteristics of interest. In most cases, these cells are the same as those used for sample selection.

For establishments that refuse, or are unable to provide data for a specific occupation, a similar cell approach is used to make adjustments to the sampled occupation weights in responding establishments. The characteristics of interest include the major occupation group of the unreported occupations.

Data on some benefit areas, such as paid sick leave and flexible benefits, did not meet publication standards. They are expected to be published in the future.

## Availability of Survey Data

The tables published in this bulletin present the major findings of the National Compensation Survey about employee benefits in private industry establishments. Survey data are also available in research articles, special bulletins and reports, and short publications. These research materials have been published in *Compensation and Working Conditions*, a quarterly publication that can be accessed online at **http://www.bls.gov/opub/cwc/cwchome.htm**, or in the *Monthly Labor Review*, which can be accessed at **http://www.bls.gov/opub/mlr/mlrhome.htm**. Both periodicals can be searched by topic using the online index.

**Table A-2. Number of establishments and part-time occupational quotes studied and estimated number of part-time workers within scope of survey, private industry, National Compensation Survey, 2000**

| Industry division[1] | Number of establishments studied | Number of occupational quotes studied[2] | | | |
|---|---|---|---|---|---|
| | | Total | Professional, technical, and related | Clerical and sales | Blue-collar and service |
| All industries ............................ | 1,436 | 951 | 170 | 342 | 439 |
| Manufacturing ....................... | 230 | 19 | 1 | 5 | 13 |
| Nonmanufacturing ................ | 1,206 | 932 | 169 | 337 | 426 |
| Mining ............................... | 10 | 1 | - | - | 1 |
| Construction ...................... | 103 | 6 | - | 2 | 4 |
| Transportation, communications, electric, gas, and sanitary services ......... | 108 | 38 | 1 | 17 | 20 |
| Wholesale trade ............... | 98 | 22 | 2 | 6 | 14 |
| Retail trade ....................... | 210 | 341 | 11 | 156 | 174 |
| Finance, insurance, and real estate ................... | 204 | 81 | 4 | 62 | 15 |
| Services ........................... | 473 | 443 | 151 | 94 | 198 |
| | | Estimated number of part-time workers within scope of survey | | | |
| All industries ............................ | | 21,598,520 | 2,452,695 | 7,440,166 | 11,705,659 |
| Manufacturing ................... | | 746,244 | 42,813 | 88,657 | 614,774 |
| Nonmanufacturing ................ | | 20,852,276 | 2,409,882 | 7,351,509 | 11,090,885 |
| Mining ............................... | | 10,693 | - | - | 10,693 |
| Construction ...................... | | 129,714 | - | 34,770 | 94,945 |
| Transportation, communications, electric, gas, and sanitary services ......... | | 1,085,261 | 5,011 | 277,121 | 803,129 |
| Wholesale trade ............... | | 596,948 | 61,218 | 135,613 | 400,117 |
| Retail trade ....................... | | 9,890,429 | 353,941 | 4,190,897 | 5,345,591 |
| Finance, insurance, and real estate ................... | | 728,287 | 56,882 | 504,819 | 166,585 |
| Services ........................... | | 8,410,944 | 1,932,829 | 2,208,290 | 4,269,825 |

[1] As defined in the 1987 edition of the *Standard Industrial Classification Manual*, U.S. Office of Management and Budget. Industry data are shown for informational purposes only and are subject to larger than normal sample error. See section on reliability of estimates.

[2] These figures refer to all respondents to the survey, whether or not they provided data for all items studied. See the section on survey response.

NOTE: Because of rounding, sums of individual items may not equal totals. Where applicable, dash indicates no employees in this category, or data do not meet publication criteria.

# *Need Wage Data Fast?*

The National Compensation Survey's **Wage Public Data Query System** has dramatically simplified the process of obtaining wage data. Searching through many printed publications for wage data is a thing of the past. The Wage Query System accesses published occupational wage data as well as modeled estimates. Published estimates are those tabulated directly from the collected data. All published estimates have been reviewed and meet BLS publication standards. Modeled estimates are derived from linear regression techniques and use coefficients to obtain a modeled hourly wage estimate. These are provided in the event published estimates are not available.

## How the Wage Query System works:

**STEP 1** — Go to http://www.bls.gov/ncs/home.htm and under Create Customized Tables select Wages (NCS) from the menu (this program requires a Java-enabled browser and takes a few moments to load)

**STEP 2** — **Select how to view the data** - occupations by area or areas by occupation

**STEP 3** — **Select an area** - view metropolitan areas, census divisions, and the nation

**STEP 4** — **Select an occupation** - up to 480 different occupations available

**STEP 5** — **Select a work level** - users can select specific work levels (1-15) and overall averages (no work level) for many occupations

### OR

**Select "Get help choosing a work level"** to view the 10 leveling factors used in producing work levels. For each factor, select the description that best describes the occupation; the system will then calculate a work level based on your answers.

**STEP 6** — **Select "Get Data"** for one query;
**Select "Add to Your Selection"** for additional queries

**Information you will receive on the data page includes:** area, occupation, level, data source (published or modeled), mean hourly wage, and reference period (year and month).

---

**For more information on the Wage Query System please contact:**
Telephone: (202) 691-6199
E-mail: ocltinfo@bls.gov

# BLS Internet Addresses

Bureau of Labor Statistics ............................................................ www.bls.gov
Division of Information Services .............................................. www.bls.gov/opub/opbinfo.htm
BLS Regional Offices ................................................................. www.bls.gov/bls/regnhome.htm

### Employment and Unemployment:
Employment, Hours, and Earnings by Industry:
    National ...................................................................... www.bls.gov/ces
    State and Area ........................................................... www.bls.gov/sae
National Labor Force Statistics .............................................. www.bls.gov/cps
Local Area Labor Force Statistics .......................................... www.bls.gov/lau
Covered Employment and Wages ......................................... www.bls.gov/cew
Occupational Employment Statistics ..................................... www.bls.gov/oes
Longitudinal Research .......................................................... www.bls.gov/nls
Job Openings and Labor Turnover ........................................ www.bls.gov/jtt

### Prices and Living Conditions:
Consumer Price Indexes ....................................................... www.bls.gov/cpi
Producer Price Indexes ......................................................... www.bls.gov/ppi
U.S. Import and Export Price Indexes ................................... www.bls.gov/mxp
Consumer Expenditure Survey .............................................. www.bls.gov/cex

### Compensation and Working Conditions:
National Compensation Survey .............................................. www.bls.gov/ncs
    Employee Benefits Survey ........................................... www.bls.gov/ncs/ebs
    Employment Cost Trends ............................................. www.bls.gov/ncs/ect
    Occupational Compensation Survey ............................ www.bls.gov/ncs/ocs
Occupational Injuries and Illnesses ....................................... www.bls.gov/iif
Collective Bargaining ........................................................... www.bls.gov/cba

### Productivity:
Quarterly Labor Productivity ................................................ www.bls.gov/lpc
Industry Productivity ............................................................ www.bls.gov/lpc
Multifactor Productivity ....................................................... www.bls.gov/mfp

### Employment Projections .............................................. www.bls.gov/emp

### International data:
Foreign Labor Statistics ........................................................ www.bls.gov/fls
U.S. Import and Export Price Indexes ................................... www.bls.gov/mxp

### All Federal Statistical Agencies

Fedstats ................................................................................ www.fedstats.gov
Firstgov ................................................................................ www.firstgov.com

*U.S. Government Printing Office: 2003—496-277/85452